Testimonials

'As a new author, I found that working with Roxanne gave me the confidence to share what I had to offer with the world! Roxanne guided me through the process, making recommendations on the structure and content where required. It was reassuring to know that I had someone in my corner all the way! I am planning my second book and will definitely be using Roxanne again.'

Jon Mailer, author of Not Just a Tradie: Time-tested principles to unlock your potential and create business freedom and flow.

'We have been working with Roxanne on a multitude of different projects over many years. Put simply, her writing and work ethic is second to absolutely none. She is the utmost professional who understands her client's needs and can work to impossible deadlines with true class. It is such a load off to know that someone will do exactly what they said they would do exactly when they said they would do it. Roxy's strength is making the author's job easy and seamless. Letting them tell the story in their own way, she weaves their words into a professional and polished manuscript. Roxy is a truly wonderful wordsmith. I highly recommend her services.'

Jody Allen, aka Stay at Home Mum, author of Earn at Home Mum, The $50 Weekly Shop: Weekday Dinners, The $50 Weekly Shop, Live Well on Less, Once a Month Cooking.

'Roxy guided me through the process of adopting an author's mindset and introduced me to the very same strategies she imparts in this book. *The Structured Author* is overflowing with practical strategies for crafting your own masterpiece, ensuring it resonates with you *and* captivates your future readers.'

Erin Lee, *author of The Little Book of Big Intentions.*

'My story would never have seen the light of day had it not been for Roxanne's passion and commitment. The means by which she gained access to my deepest and most vulnerable beliefs and stories enhanced the power of my book's message. Totally professional and always looking for ways to better support me, Roxanne didn't stop with just the ghostwriting; going the extra mile, she has included me in the extension of her business interests to ensure that my manuscript is now well on its way to becoming bestseller material.

Roxanne is so much more than even her website suggests – a mentor, innovator, visionary and business leader like few others.'

Stew Darling, *author of Lead through Life and Unstoppable: Living Beyond Your Limits.*

'Roxanne possesses an innate gift for capturing the unique voices and perspectives of others, ensuring that every story is told with the utmost respect and authenticity. Her ability to connect with the essence of each narrative and translate it into words is nothing short of extraordinary. Beyond her exceptional writing skills, Roxanne is a true collaborator. I wholeheartedly recommend *The Structured Author* to anyone seeking to infuse their writing with authenticity, emotion and, above all, passion. Roxanne has not just written a book; she has ignited a flame that will continue to burn brightly in the hearts and words of those fortunate enough to discover her wisdom.'

 Paula Gowland, *author of Legless: From Trauma to Triumph*

'Prepare to unleash your inner author with *The Structured Author*, an indispensable companion for anyone considering the journey to authorship. Roxy shares her wealth of experience as a journalist, author, author coach, and ghostwriter, leaving you in no doubt about how to plan, start, and complete that book you've always dreamt about writing. I wish I had the benefit of this book when I embarked on the journey to authorship. The book is a practical guide to finding a structure and empowering you to sculpt your ideas with precision and purpose. It's like having Roxy guide you step by step in the book writing process, walking hand in hand with you on the journey to becoming an author. After immersing myself in its pages, I'm not just inspired – I'm ready to pen my next masterpiece!'

 Kym Cousins, *author of Selling with Heart.*

IGNITE & WRITE

BOOK TWO

The Structured Author

Roxanne McCarty-O'Kane

Ignite & Write: The Structured Author
Author – Roxanne McCarty-O'Kane
© Roxanne McCarty-O'Kane 2024

www.roxannewriter.com
hello@roxannewriter.com.au

Facebook: facebook.com/roxannewriter
Instagram: @roxannewriter
LinkedIn: linkedin.com/in/roxannemccartyokane/

ABN: 62660117725

This book is sold with the understanding that the author is not offering specific, personal advice to the reader. By reading this book, you acknowledge and accept that book writing is a dynamic field, and no one-size-fits-all solution exists. It is your responsibility to evaluate the relevance and applicability of the advice provided in the context of your unique story vision.

For professional personalised advice about your book, get in touch with Roxanne directly. The author disclaims any responsibility for liability, loss or risk, personal or otherwise, arising as a consequence of the use and application of any of the contents of this book.

The information in this publication is provided for general purposes only. It is not to be relied on as a substitute for legal advice. You should at all times consult with your own lawyer, especially if your writing concerns matter before the court or for any issues regarding possible defamation.

All rights reserved. This book may not be reproduced in whole or part, stored, posted on the internet, or transmitted in any form or by any means, electronic or mechanical, or by photocopying, recording, sharing or other means, without written permission from the author of this book. All content found online or offline without written permission is in breach of copyright law and, therefore, renders you liable for damages and at risk of prosecution.

Cover illustration by Cara Ord, www.caraordcreate.com
Editing by Candice Holznagel, www.wordsbycandice.com.au
Designed by Sylvie Blair, www.bookpod.com.au
Published by Ignite & Write Publishing, www.igniteandwritepublishing.com

ISBN: 978-0-6455447-4-9 (paperback); 978-0-6455447-5-6 (ebook)

 A catalogue record for this book is available from the National Library of Australia

May you find the words to articulate everything you have on your heart and in your mind.

Let go and allow your story to truly shine.

Contents

A note from Roxy	1
Time to ACT	13
Mind mapping	19
Nonfiction subgenres	27
Structure	53
Creating your manuscript structure	67
Chapter structure	75
Writing	81
Beating writer's block	133
Product vs pillar	145
Beyond the SFD	165
The pep talk	187
Acknowledgments	195
About Roxy	197
References	200
The Ignite & Write Trilogy	202

A note from Roxy

The seatbelt cuts into my neck as I strain to see out of the rear window. My cheeks are soaked as my insides twist like the plait Mum weaves into my hair every night to keep the knots at bay.

Why did you do that? Why couldn't you just have listened?

The car pulls away, and through blurred vision, I watch as my dad becomes smaller and smaller, even though he is running as fast as he can to try and catch us. I don't remember many things. I have a goldfish memory that would rival even the likes of Pixar's beloved blue tang Dory. But this memory is etched into my soul. It was the day I told myself that I should never speak up.

I would have been seven or eight at the time, old enough to think I was ten-foot-tall, bulletproof and knew more about the world than my parents. I had been at a dragon boat racing carnival with Dad, who I got to see every fortnight. My parents divorced when I was two. By the time I was in upper primary school, I had a stepfather and two younger half-brothers, not that I ever called them that. It feels icky even using the word 'step' because I have never experienced anything other than unconditional love and inclusion from the man who married my Mum and committed to raising me as well. They were just Dad and my brothers.

Ignite & Write: The Structured Author

I was surrounded by love, but it was hard navigating two different households, two sets of expectations, two different value and belief systems, two opposing lists of rules. I did my best to smile and be happy, but there were many nights when I poured my heart out into the pages of my diary because I didn't want anyone to know how much it hurt to be the odd one out, never really fitting perfectly into one household or the other. I want to be clear no one ever made me feel that way; it was how I made sense of the world in my young mind.

On this particular day, Dad was competing in the racing carnival. I'd stayed in the team tent on the Wellington foreshore with the support crew, reading my book, eating my fill of snacks and watching what I could from the shade. But I could see a park filled with children and as the hours passed, I wanted nothing more than to go over there and play.

With another heat coming up, I asked Dad if I could go. He refused, but I pleaded. 'I'll be fine, it's right there. I'll go straight there and come straight back. I won't talk to anyone or go anywhere else...' *I think that covers all the bases*. He seemed unsure, but as I continued to present my case for how responsible I was, he finally relented.

I skipped over to the park and climbed up the towering white spire to wait for my turn on the slide. I had no concept of time; my fractured memory would say it was only a few minutes before I saw one of my younger brothers. A smile spread across my face as I ran up to say hi. As I made my way down the slide, I ran to Mum for a hug.

A note from Roxy

'Who are you here with?' she asked with surprise, craning her neck to look around the sea of strangers in an attempt to seek out a familiar face.

'Dad.'

'Where is he?'

'He's racing. I'm just here for a bit and then I'll go back to the team tent...' *Oh no.*

'Who's watching you?' I could see her anger rise and knew I was in trouble. *I wish I'd hidden instead; what was I thinking?*

Before I could fully process what was happening, I was told to get in the car. I didn't want to leave; I was having fun, and it was my weekend with Dad. I don't know how he found out what was happening, but I remember his look of shock as he chased after the car. I was driven back to Mum's with no idea if I would ever see him again.

As a parent myself now, I can fully appreciate Mum's reaction. I was a child, unsupervised in a city park. I can also appreciate my dad's decision to cave, only having me fifty-two days a year, he wasn't as well practised at standing firm – an example of the two different rules and values.

As a child, I blamed myself for all of it. As a result, I chose to be selective on when I spoke up, and more often than not, I didn't. I dampened my voice out of fear I would do something wrong and hurt the people around me again.

Ignite & Write: The Structured Author

The joy of life is that we accumulate new experiences every day, and when we take the time, we can discover new things about ourselves every day, too. I used to think I knew myself incredibly well… then I decided to write a book. It makes you look back on your life as an observer for the first time, a powerful gift that so many don't give to themselves.

In *The Mindful Author*, Book One of the *Ignite & Write Trilogy*, along with introducing you to my ACT process, I shared the journey that led me down the path to becoming a multi-award-winning nonfiction book ghostwriter, writing mentor, workshop facilitator, presenter and MC.

But I would be remiss to launch straight into showing you how to structure your book without updating that journey for you. As a former journalist, I know that 'why' is often the most powerful question you can ask in any situation, yet it was one I had failed to ask myself on a deeper level until 2022.

Needless to say, I have peeled back another few layers of myself since I published my first book. I have taken some time to examine why I was drawn to journalism as a career and ghostwriting as a business.

It was never to have my name up in lights, to have access to areas of the world most people don't, or to be able to ask anyone in an interview – no matter what their status in society – any question on my mind in the name of public interest (whether they answered or not was never guaranteed!). I'm not going to lie, the last two were pretty cool, but they weren't driving forces for me.

A note from Roxy

So what was?

In 2022 I enrolled in the inaugural Lionhearted Foundation Leadership Course with the intention to strengthen my self-belief as a leader. The facilitator, Jeanette Allom-Hill, is someone whom I admired as a strong leader who had an equal balance of grace and grit. As I learned about the concept of Ikigai – the Japanese ethos of living with purpose – I realised that I needed to dig deeper.

I already knew my purpose. I had found how I could use my skills as a storyteller to serve the world and had been doing so since 2007. But there was one niggling question – *why* was I drawn into that world?

As you know from Book One, I was on track for a career in the Air Force until the universe stepped in and blocked my path when I failed an additional physical test given to people with a history of asthma. I was devastated at the time, but with the power of hindsight, I know it was what I needed to go through in order to find my place in a career and a business that made me genuinely happy.

> It's challenging to step back into your past to revisit people, events and emotions.

I see my clients bravely venture through this every day and it is nothing short of inspiring. I used to smirk when I heard the phrase, 'Everything stems from your childhood'. It seems so cringeworthily cliché, but without a better idea of how I could answer my question, I started there.

I may have already been a people pleaser, an overachiever, someone who would consider every single decision for far too long, overanalysing everything in case the one that I made had a negative impact on someone else, but the dragonboat carnival event only served to amplify that.

Slowly but surely, I suppressed parts of myself. At school, I was always the best friend of the popular girl, but I never put myself out there as being worthy enough to be popular myself. I hid. I was afraid to stand up for myself, even when I felt wronged. Instead, I would vent in my diary or to a close friend, sometimes to Mum, to get things off my chest, but rarely did I ever address things directly with the person who had hurt me.

I had lost sight of the power of my voice.

I know where you might think this is going, but no, journalism didn't help me find my voice. It helped me to empower others to find theirs. That was enough to light me up and sustain me for the first twelve years of my career. Is it enough for me now? No. But what I've come to know is that the universe only gives you what you can handle at any given moment.

There was much more I had to see, feel and experience before I was ready to face my unexpected redundancy. Well, let's be honest, I didn't really face it. I was summoned into the editorial office of the newspaper company I'd spent the better part of a decade working at. I'd spent the day as I did every other day at work, chasing down interviews, organising photo shoots, writing

A note from Roxy

and uploading news stories to the system for online readers and preparing separate files for the next day's print version.

I was perplexed as I saw not only my editor but some guy I'd never seen before sitting on the opposite side of the table. I can only imagine the blank expression I had on my face as I sat down. The editor began talking, 'Blah blah blah... sorry... blah blah blah... restructure... blah blah blah... we're letting you go.'

The strange guy pushed some papers towards me, 'We've worked out a redundancy package that reflects your time here. We believe you will find it fair.'

I blinked. Can you guess what the first words out of my mouth were?

'What have I done wrong?'

That inner child who was so desperate to please and do the right thing felt like she'd just been reprimanded and told she was the most unworthy human on Earth. I didn't stand up for myself. I was left at the table in tears and told that I could pack up my things and go when I was ready.

The nine-to-five was all I knew, and with print editions being phased out quicker than Paris Hilton changes outfits, I didn't rate my chances of continuing as a journalist. But I opened myself up to whatever opportunities were out there and found my first freelance opportunity just two weeks after being made redundant. I was running my own business!

Ignite & Write: The Structured Author

It allowed me to have control over who I worked for and the hours I wanted to put in – a level of professional flexibility I had never experienced before. I had started to find my own voice and it gave me the confidence to dare to try something new – nonfiction book ghostwriting. Dozens of book titles and three awards later, I am writing this book for you.

Divine timing is something I truly believe in. If I were to be thrust into the position of having to create my own business and find my voice seven years earlier, I would have been devastated beyond repair.

By the time my redundancy came, I knew that telling people's stories and giving them a chance to share their message within the community or around the world was my superpower. I had also developed finely-honed skills so I can help people to share their truth at a high level. Sharing real-life knowledge and experience is what lights me up more than creating fantastical fictional worlds because I know the power of building collective knowledge and wisdom by passing our stories down. When they are captured in book form, they are there for posterity. So, here we are.

It might seem a bit self-indulgent that I've dedicated pages to sharing this self-discovery with you, but there is a purpose behind it. Yes, this too is a teachable moment. Without knowing my true 'why' and what lies underneath the many layers that drive my subconscious thoughts and actions, I was only half present.

A note from Roxy

When you can dig to the bottom of your 'why,' you will become unstoppable.

This is the book that will empower you to take your dream of being a nonfiction author and turn that into a verb. It's time to kick into high gear, ditch the excuses, and take action to make your book a reality.

I know you have a book inside of you. You know you have a book inside of you. This is why we are here. You may have felt a calling for many years to begin to share your story, or perhaps it is a relatively new pursuit for you. Either way, the writing journey you are about to embark on is a life-changing experience and it will be yours if you stay the course and see your vision through.

I'm not going to sugar-coat this, becoming an author takes a lot of time and effort, but I know that many aspiring authors do not even manage to take the first step. Uncertainty over what to do, when to do it and how to do it does nothing but hold people back from their goals.

But you are different.

You have already taken that first step by buying this book (possibly having already read Book One – go you!). The second step by opening the cover and the third step by taking the time to read the content, which will provide you with a map for your journey. You are well on your way, so keep up the momentum!

Ignite & Write: The Structured Author

This book will take you through the writing process with some useful tips and tricks to help you stay in flow, as well as walking you through building a structure to work to. This might seem like a tedious process, but believe me, it is some of the wisest time you will invest in your authorship journey because it will help you to become focused and able to proceed with clarity.

Book Three is dedicated to what comes after you have finished that first draft: publishing and marketing your book to make it the success you have dreamed of.

The steps forward are clear and easy to manage and you will feel more empowered than ever before to achieve your dream. You will also feel more connected to yourself, your story and your audience, which will propel you through any future hurdles to becoming the author you deserve to be.

I am beyond excited to take you on this journey!

Roxanne McCarty-O'Kane

A note from Roxy

> *'Use the power of your word in the direction of truth and love.'*
>
> Don Miguel Ruiz, author
> and spiritual teacher.

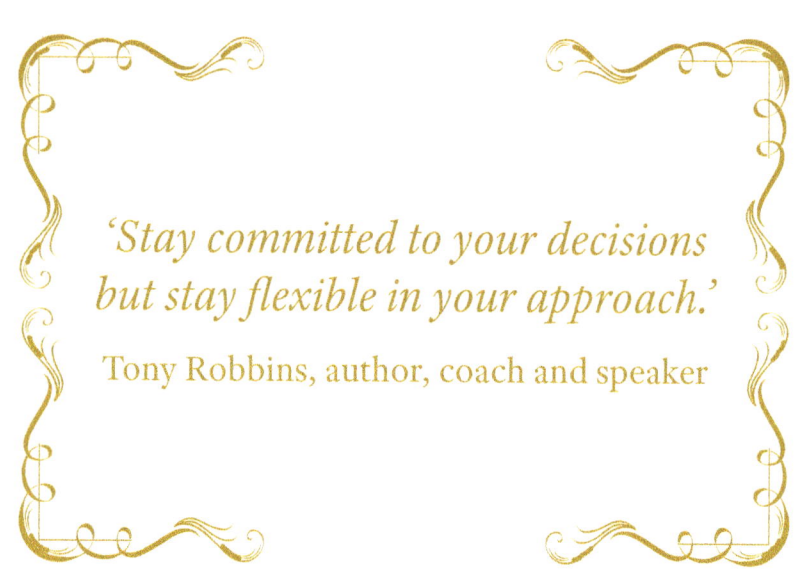

'Stay committed to your decisions but stay flexible in your approach.'

Tony Robbins, author, coach and speaker

Time to ACT

Ignite & Write: The Structured Author

I cringe every time I see a post in a social media group from an aspiring author who is looking for advice on where to start. The most common response is, 'Just write!' Yes, it's true that you will actually need to write in order to reach your goal, *but* real success lies in having strong foundations and a structure in place.

When people try to write on their own without structure, it usually goes one of two ways, and I have witnessed this time and time again when people come to me for help:

1. You start off absolutely gunning it, writing down all your memories and anecdotes, sharing wisdom and ways in which you or your businesses have grown. You toil for hours on end, feeling increasingly excited as you get closer and closer to the word count you have set for yourself. When you finally hit the magic milestone, you finish with a huge sigh of relief and celebrate. It sounds ideal, right? But for the aspiring author who writes with no structure, this means:

     The manuscript contains tens of thousands of words with zero structure and order. The content might be great, but the reader can't follow a logical path to piece everything together in a way that makes sense and shares a strong message. Because of this, connection is lacking.

     You will be up for a much larger editing bill. With a professional editor on board, they will have to wade through all of your content and rework it in order to bring that all-important structure around the words.

 The editor may find large sections of irrelevant copy that can't actually be used in the book, meaning time and energy have been wasted creating it in the first place. This can be crushing when you have poured your heart and soul into writing your manuscript.

These may be simple blips for some writers who are able to overcome these hurdles with gusto. But for others, these are devastating blows that can be enough for them to shelve their book forever.

2. You are stuck from day one because you are unable to write without a clear path forward and are unsure of how to actually pave that path. You may take a few stilted attempts at writing but find writing without a clear purpose sees you spending time staring at the wall or writing yourself into a corner with no way forward. This means:

 The time you spend is unproductive and lacks focus.

 Frustration at the lack of progress quickly kicks in, followed by an amplification of those negative voices we covered in detail in Book One, *The Mindful Author*.

More often than not, it is uncertainty and the accompanying feeling of stagnation that will kick any motivation you once had to the curb.

Do you see yourself in either of those scenarios? As you can imagine, neither of those aspiring authors has a happy ending. I may see some of them years down the track when they come to me and ask for assistance with restructuring. I can then help them to identify a clear way to present their stories. But for every person who does take action down the track, I bet there would be thousands more who simply give up and walk away. That breaks my heart because the stories they were once so passionate about sharing will never see the light of day. Those unique insights will not have the opportunity to be out there in the world where they have the potential to make a difference.

Since you are here, that won't be you.

You understand the importance of having a structure in place.

The Mindful Author focused on building strong foundations for your book. If you haven't already, I highly recommend that you read Book One before continuing with Book Two, as it will help you to determine your driving force – your 'why' – and shape a profile of who your ideal reader is. You will then understand how your book can be valuable to them.

Using the exercises from Book One, can you articulate:

 your authentic voice?

 what is your 'why' for writing your book?

Time to ACT

 who is your ideal reader?
 what is your book vision?

With these foundations in place, you have everything you need to build your book structure. As you progress through this book, we will revisit the method of ACT – Authenticity, Connection and Transformation – with new questions, including:

 Authenticity – What are the major milestones of your life?
 Connection – What do you want to share with your ideal reader?
 Transformation – How do you want to transform through this process? What about your ideal reader? What would you like to see them achieve?

The book in your hands right now is the next step to guide you through how to pull all of this together to build a skeleton structure for your book manuscript. I call it a skeleton structure because it holds the basic information you can use as a guide to flesh out your book.

It is also super important to realise that this structure is not immovable. In fact, I encourage you to make it as fluid as possible because writing is a creative process. If you try to fix too many rules around it, you could be blocking the potential for surprising and unexpected insights to land in your lap as you open yourself up to the process.

Let's not waste a moment longer!

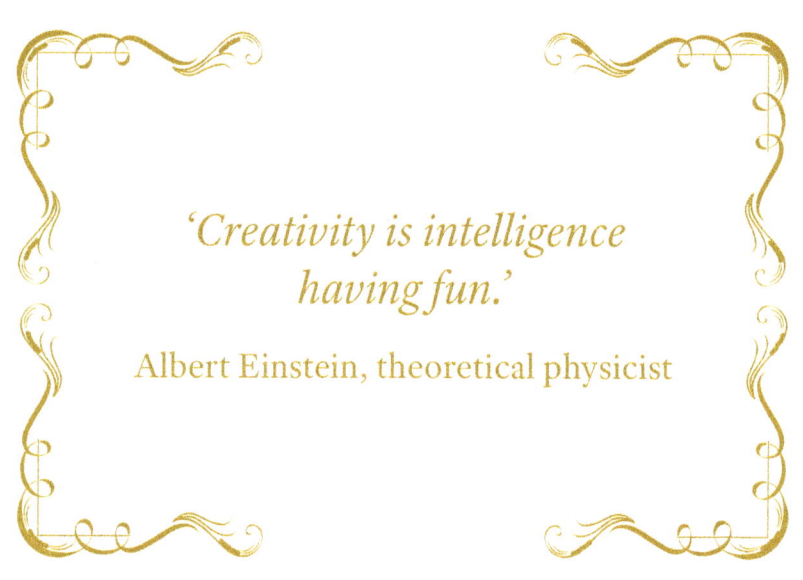

'Creativity is intelligence having fun.'

Albert Einstein, theoretical physicist

Mind mapping

Ignite & Write: The Structured Author

How would you feel if I asked you to write down the structure of your book from start to finish right now?

Chances are, you would feel stressed. *Wait! I don't even know what I want to say yet!* Perfectionism would kick in. *What if I write something down for chapter one and then realise three more chapters need to come before that?* Then the overwhelm. *But there is so much to cover; where do I start?*

The system that we are going to tap into as I take you through the process of structuring your book is called the mind map. Now, this is certainly not my invention. It has been around for centuries.

You may not yet know the name Tony Buzan, but he is the author and educational consultant credited with popularising the mind map. Buzan was a British television personality who was nominated for two Nobel Peace Prizes, wrote eighty books and travelled the world showing people how to organise their thoughts and structure information through mapping.[1]

While Buzan is credited with popularising the concept, taking a blank page and adding a concept in the middle with images, words and colours surrounding it dates back centuries earlier. Philosopher Ramon Llull also using similar techniques during his lifetime in Majorca from 1235-1315.[2]

As you can see, the design of the mind map is such that there are layers. The central concept branches out to major ideas, and those major ideas have smaller, minor ideas linked to them. When I first played around with the idea of using mind maps for book

Mind mapping

structure, I would ask the aspiring authors in my workshop to do a single *huge* brain dump to get everything out of their minds.

The result was that they quickly fell into overwhelm. So, in this book, I will show you the strategy I employ that *works* because it allows you to add layer after layer, focusing on one element at a time, in order to build a comprehensive map.

Once all the steps are complete, you will be able to follow through with creating a cohesive structure – yes, it's a list! Essentially, we are allowing your creative and analytical mind to run free together through the mapping process in order to create this list, which will become your invaluable skeleton structure. With this, you will be able to write with clarity and focus whenever you snatch some precious moments to write your book content.

Mind maps are effective because they engage both sides of the brain simultaneously.

When we begin to write a traditional list to gather our thoughts, we engage the functional part of the brain – the right side. In comparison, a mind map, with its limitless combinations and ability to move away from fully formed sentences and incorporate single words, feelings, images and colours, calls on the creative left side as well.

This opens up your thought process exponentially, allowing you to see new and exciting connections within your story and how you can present your ideas and knowledge to your reader. You may be surprised at what you can come up with when you apply the mind map concept to your book.

So, guess what? That's exactly what we're going to do now.

Creating your mind map

Grab a large piece of paper. I'm talking bigger than the A4 you likely have stored in your cupboards. Head down to the local newsagent and get an A3 or even an A2-sized piece of paper or cardboard. The bigger, the better! The last thing you want to do is restrict your thoughts. This is an exciting project, and you want to have the space you need to let your creativity run wild.

There are online forms of mind mapping you can access if you prefer, but there is something about sitting down and creating

Mind mapping

something by hand that makes the process flow much more intuitively for me.

Also, make sure you have colour in the form of pencils, markers or even crayons. At a pinch, you could even resort to rustling up multiple pens in the traditional blue, red, green and black varieties; anything that will allow you to spruce up your page and tap into the creative element.

Before you sit down to do this, try to create the type of environment you enjoy. It could be setting up outside under a tree or taking a picnic blanket to the beach and dipping your toes in the sand. For me, it's playing music that I love and lighting a candle that fills the room with a gorgeous scent.

When you sit down to mind map, try to clear your mind as much as possible. Remember, there is no right or wrong way to mind map, so kick that perfectionist brain to the curb. This is the time to play!

Whatever comes through your pen is perfectly perfect, and while it might not make sense the moment the thought pops into your mind, write it down anyway because you may be surprised at how relevant it may become as the overall picture begins to take shape.

We will come back to this mind map throughout the book, so keep it in a place that is easy to access as you journey through the process of building your chapter structure.

Whenever you see this symbol: you know it's time to grab your mind map.

Ignite & Write: The Structured Author

MAP IT OUT

With your central concept in place, it's time to work with the foundations you built in Book One. You might like to assign each of these a different colour so you can easily connect the dots and align elements from different categories later on. Choose a colour for each of the following:

- thoughts for your ideal reader
- thoughts for your ideal client (if relevant)
- frameworks or processes
- personal stories or lifetime milestones
- professional stories or business milestones
- quotes or lyrics that have inspired or guided you.

Let's start to build your mind map.

1. As you have seen in the example, start your mind map with the central concept in the middle. If you have a working title for your book, you can put this here. Don't worry if it hasn't come to you yet; some authors are still trying to come up with 'the one' while the book is being designed! If the inspiration hasn't landed for you yet, place the theme of your book in the middle, or simply write 'My Book'.

2. Consider your 'why'. What elements of your authentic story are relevant to the purpose of your

Mind mapping

book? These will become the major concepts or branches. You don't need to be detailed; simple dot points are perfect for capturing your thoughts without diving too deep down each rabbit hole. Think about each pivotal moment of your story and pop it onto its own branch on the map.

3. Consider your ideal reader and take a bird's eye view of your lived experience and knowledge. What would you like to share with them? This could include other elements of your lived experience, the highs and the lows. Give each one its own branch.

4. If your book has a business or education component, consider your ideal client. What would you like to share with them? This could include a professional framework or process or even case studies. Give each one its own branch.

Don't worry if you only have a few items at this stage; we are just getting started. The more you work through this book, the more clarity you will receive on your message and the more confident you will become in just writing everything down as it comes to you (yes, I see you holding back because you still aren't sure you are doing it 'right'! Remember, there is no right or wrong.)

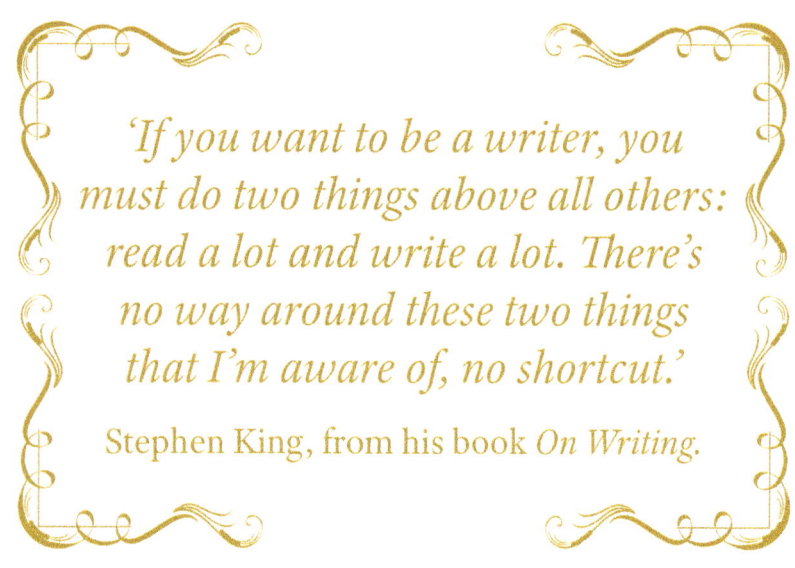

'If you want to be a writer, you must do two things above all others: read a lot and write a lot. There's no way around these two things that I'm aware of, no shortcut.'

Stephen King, from his book *On Writing*.

Nonfiction subgenres

Ignite & Write: The Structured Author

Congratulations! You have completed the first layer of your mind map. Before we refine your map any further, I feel it's important to demystify the different nonfiction genres and what is available to you. Nonfiction is a genre, sure, but within that genre, there are many subgenres. Knowing what they are will empower you to choose a style of book that best fits your style of story.

Please don't view this as an exercise in pigeon-holing your book (you will see there are many ways to make your book exactly how you envisioned it) but more as a means of eliminating the genres that don't feel right to you so you can be more focused in how you write.

Identifying the specific genre of your book assists in a number of ways. Having an understanding will help when it comes time to categorise your book for marketing and listing on platforms such as Amazon, which require you to select two categories for your book.

Secondly, self-connection to your genre is vital in producing a book that will resonate with your readers. I have lost count of the number of aspiring authors who have thought the answer to all their problems would be found by openly sharing their truth in a 'faction' book. This is one that is based on fact but is sprinkled with fiction. Others want to go full fiction.

But as Australian journalist, editor, and award-winning author Leigh Robshaw shared on the *Ignite & Write* podcast (formerly *The Phoenix Phenomenon)*, being unclear on how you want to present your story can delay your ability to communicate your story in a way that feels authentic and that connects with your readers. It took Leigh seven years to turn her original idea for *You Had Me at Hola* into a physical book she could hold in her hands. Here's why:

> 'I loved *The Alchemist* by Paulo Coelho, the Brazilian writer, and I wanted to emulate that fable-type style. I started writing in that sort of fabley tone, and it just didn't seem right. I stuck with it on and off for seven years. I would do a bit, and then I'd put it away for long periods of time. Then one day, I said, 'That's it. I'm just going to sit down and write it as if I was writing to a friend and see if the writing will come out as naturally as possible if I do it that way'. Once I did that, everything changed. I realised my commitment was to the story, above what people think of me and what I've done or what my friends and family thought of me writing this. It just sort of paled into comparison when I thought the most important thing for my soul really was to be true to this story. The more I did that, the more it flowed.'

Instead of trying to hide her lived experience behind a fictionalised character and version of real-life events, Leigh discovered freedom in being able to present her story in its genuine form – a memoir. Leigh self-published *You Had Me at Hola*, and it was so well received that a traditional publishing house took on her second book.

You can listen to Leigh's full interview here:

Ignite & Write: The Structured Author

If you are in doubt whether you would like to create a work of nonfiction or fiction, I suggest you revisit the 'why' you uncovered from Book One. Is your 'why' anchored in:

- educating and sharing knowledge
- inspiring positive change or action in your readers
- cautioning your readers through sharing your lived experience?

If so, you will convey your message much more powerfully in a nonfiction book. When readers pick up a novel or work of fiction, they settle in for entertainment. If they are lucky, they may take away something new from the experience. But when you can share your truth from a place of authenticity and take your readers on the journey that you have lived, your message resounds clearer and stronger.

This is why I am so passionate about supporting aspiring nonfiction authors like you. I want to help you find your authentic voice and to share your message in the most powerful way possible. Now, when venturing into this unfamiliar world of writing, clarity is of the utmost importance. Once you know that nonfiction is the path you would like to travel, it's time to refine which subgenre of nonfiction is going to allow your style of story to truly shine.

To help you find the best fit for your book format and genre, here is a rundown of the largest categories within the nonfiction realm.

Nonfiction subgenres

Autobiography

I am often asked what the difference is between a memoir and an autobiography. You may be inclined to lump them into the same basket, but there is a small distinction between the two that sets them worlds apart in the literary world.

An autobiography is a book that tells the life story of the author from childhood all the way through to the time of writing – capturing all of the major milestones and events that have led them to where they are today.

Autobiographies can give you incredible insight into people's lives. They open closed doors and invite you into the most intimate scenarios. You discover things people outside of the author's personal network never knew about.

By sharing these experiences, autobiographies create an incredibly strong connection between the author and the reader. The readers now understand more about them and have more empathy and trust.

The first autobiography I ever read was Nelson Mandela's *Long Walk to Freedom*. It's a daily habit now for me to work my way through the growing list of autobiographies being released each year. As a writer, it gives me further insight into how people present their stories and the types of writing trends that are emerging so I can perfect my craft. Two of my more recent favourites were Dave Grohl's insightful *The Storyteller* and Matthew McConaughey's *Greenlights*.

Books by the likes of socialite Paris Hilton and actor Elliot Page, which were released in 2023, allowed me to break through any preconceptions I had about both celebrity figures. Both unapologetically took readers by the hand to openly share the most traumatic experiences of their lives.

You don't have to be a celebrity to release an autobiography.

Everyday heroes, like the late Holocaust survivor and author of *The Happiest Man on Earth*, Eddie Jaku, can write incredibly impactful books that change lives.

As you will discover, writing an autobiography doesn't mean you have to start with the moment you arrived in the world and end with the present day. You can play around with the introduction chapter and apply a circular structure to get readers excited about what awaits them as they learn everything about you. We will cover more about this structure later in this book.

So, what about the differences between biography and *auto*biography?

They are both books about someone's life, but the primary difference here is a biography is written by someone other than the subject of the book. An autobiography, on the other hand, is written by the actual person. There is a small caveat here – many of your favourite celebrity autobiographies are not penned by the person on the front cover! Unless they have a hidden literary prowess or have had a large chunk of time away

Nonfiction subgenres

from their careers to sit down and write, it is likely they have used a ghostwriter to help them craft their stories in a powerful and engaging way.

You will see some celeb books use 'with' and have the name of their ghostwriter (often called co-writers in this instance) on the front cover, or you may see nothing at all. That is the beauty of engaging ghosties like myself; you do not have to disclose that ghostwriters are involved in the creation of your book if you do not wish to.

Memoir

In contrast, a memoir is a powerful subgenre for someone who may want to focus on a specific period of time or a single theme. A great example of a well-executed memoir that became an international bestseller is Elizabeth Gilbert's *Eat Pray Love*. This covered her years of self-discovery following divorce and the international travel that led to her accepting herself and healing her past wounds.

Memoir themes are limitless and can capture periods of time during:

- your profession or career
- a relationship
- a health battle, such as a cancer diagnosis
- a life-changing holiday
- living through a disaster, either natural or manmade, such as war.

For the story approach, think of the book as sharing a single chapter of your life. Ask yourself, when did that chapter begin? When did it end? What did the hero learn along the way? How will it benefit your readers? Having a container around what you're going to share will help you stay on track.

You will be surprised to learn that readers don't need copious amounts of backstory to be able to follow your journey. All you need to do is give them the relevant breadcrumbs.

Memoirs can cover multiple seasons of someone's life, but the events covered are always linked to a central theme that is developed throughout the book. To execute a great memoir, you need to be clear on a single message you want to share or a story you want to tell in order to be able to share the experiences that are relevant to that message.

Some ideas could include:

- loss or creation of wealth
- escaping a domestic violence situation
- overcoming some form of physical or emotional trauma
- a major life event
- finding religion or spirituality.

How-to/Self-help

How-to and self-help are quite broad categories. When you boil it down, the how-to subgenre is generally linked with teaching specific skills, while a self-help book is geared towards personal development.

Both are prescriptive in the way they communicate information, which can be great for aspiring authors who are fans of to-do lists and being able to tick things off in a logical order. This style of book suits step-by-step instructions and frameworks that readers are expected to follow to achieve the outcome you want to give them.

There is a myriad of examples or topics you could draw from:

- building a million-dollar business
- leadership
- financial independence
- living a healthier lifestyle
- tapping into spirituality.

Listicles

This was a term we used heavily in the newsroom towards the end of my time as a journalist and was used to describe stories that were based on lists. For journos, these topics ranged from the Top 10 tips for holidaying with children to the Top 100 influencers in the region. It was actually one of my few pet peeves about where media was headed at the time because I found listicles presented as news had close to zero value… but that's a debate for another time.

However, this formula is popular in the nonfiction book realm, especially where simplicity is the goal. There was an era around the early 2010s when there seemed to be a war on how many 'tips' you could provide to your readers. The standard 10, 20 or 50 gave way to odd and unexpected numbers like 72, 157 or even 1001. It was comical to see the numbers rise as authors worked hard to outdo each other in the 'value' they were providing.

However, the danger of going too high with your tip count is that you have less space to cover each point. The target market for a book such as this would likely desire quick, easy tips. Writing even a couple of hundred words for each of the 100 tips, for example, would create a gigantic tome that would be off-putting.

Also, having too many tips or list items can force you into generic territory or repetition of similar points, which can lead to the reader feeling taken advantage of. A book based around 10 tips where you can do a deep dive into each one could be far more effective than trying to stretch that out to 100. With the latter, you may be forced to dream up weird or not so relevant tips to make up the goal number you've set for yourself.

If you have a very specific ideal reader and a wealth of knowledge to draw on, this could be an ideal way to channel your content into an easy-to-read book.

Collaborative

The hot trend to emerge in the 2020s was most definitely the collaborative book. It works on a number of levels. Firstly, you are able to bring a variety of voices and perspectives into a single book. Secondly, the writing workload is reduced significantly if people contribute their own chapters. Thirdly, you have a head start on your marketing because each of your contributors will want the book to succeed and will be so proud of their involvement that they will be spreading the word as well.

I have been fortunate to have been featured in two collaborative books. The first is called *SHINE'ing the Spotlight*, which was collated and edited by Sunshine Coast businesswoman and mentor Zoe Sparks. This book was released in 2019 and featured my story alongside 51 other amazing businesswomen. Every week for a year, Zoe had been profiling businesswomen in her SHINE Business Women newsletter. This was done by sending out questionnaires to women she wished to feature and then sending small profiles to her subscribers and posting them to social media.

Once she had amassed a year's worth of content, Zoe decided to edit the profiles further and collate them into a book, which became another pillar of her business network. The launch was an incredible night with many of the 52 women turning up for the milestone and all of us actively promoting the book going forward.

The second collaborative book I have featured in is called *How to Become Your Best Version: Wisdom Shared by the Women of the Becoming Your Best Version Podcast* by Maria Leonard Olsen.[3] The US-based author, attorney, public speaker, podcaster and book marketing coach created a successful international podcast that has become a powerful platform for women to share stories of triumph and overcoming adversity and how they became the best version of themselves despite their challenges.

Already a multi-time author, Maria knew that the stories shared needed to reach more people and launched her book in order to tap into a different audience of global readers. The powerful combination of podcast and book has proven to be incredibly successful.

Both Zoe and Maria already had the content they needed to repurpose for their books (with permission from their interviewees, of course). This goes to show that your contributors don't necessarily have to write their own chapters. In fact, you may prefer to write chapters for them or have them write something with your guidance on the type of content you are looking for (as long as you get final editorial say on what is published of course).

A client I have had the privilege of working on two collaborative books with is Kerrie Atherton, who is the founder of the international Stories of HOPE, CEO of EMPOWER Life Solutions, keynote speaker, author, mental health first aid training presenter, and a trauma and addictions recovery counsellor. Kerrie released *Stories of HOPE: Everyday People, Extraordinary Stories* and *Stories of HOPE: Resilient People, Remarkable Stories*. Each featured eleven stories from contributing authors and a chapter from Kerrie, who shared different poignant moments from her own life.

Kerrie is a classic connector who established Stories of Hope in 2017 and has two speakers at her free monthly community events. The speakers would cover all types of stories of hope, from financial to health challenges, addiction, mental health and relationship battles. She built a strong community around her events, and her books, which feature some of the most popular stories, are designed to spread those messages of hope far beyond the local region.

You can choose whether you foot the bill for the creation of the book and, therefore, have all of the returns once books are selling or request that each contributor pay a set fee to cover their portion of the production costs and become entitled to a percentage of the sales. There are many different ways you can structure it to suit, but it is vital that all of this is clear from the outset so you are managing expectations and laying the legal foundations for clarity for all parties.

Academic

Books that require a lot of research generally fall into their own category. You have historical narratives, of course, but when you are focused solely on educating and have a niche academic audience, the style in which you write and present your book is going to be different to one that is designed for the layperson.

Like how-to and self-help books, academic-style books are prescriptive in how they are presented. Think university assignment style with an introduction, each chapter having a basic outline of the topic, hypothesis, theory, and explanation and conclusion. Of course, everything will be heavily referenced, so there needs to be an extensive collection of end notes to satisfy the requirements to backup findings and validate statistics.

This is not the style of writing that I focus on with my aspiring writers, so I won't delve much further into this subgenre.

Coffee table book

For those of you who have a highly visual market, a coffee table book that relies more heavily on imagery can be a great option. It is said that a picture is worth a thousand words, and if you work in an industry where aesthetics are everything, relying more heavily on images to tell your story is a fabulous way to go.

Another book I have featured in is *Women Inspired*, which was a collaboration between photographer Jaya McIntyre and writer Melinda Uys in 2021. They created a beautifully designed coffee table book that features a full-page photo taken by Jaya, alongside a snapshot story written by Melinda. This was a project I paid a fee for as all of the work was done for me – a lovely interview with Mel and a fun-filled photo shoot with Jaya, and the magical book was brought to life.

The launch night was a mega celebration, and the book sits proudly in my office and has been doing the rounds of independent bookshops. In a pleasant twist, I was asked by Jaya to become the book's writer in 2023, and we collaborated on bringing together forty-two women, including Olympian Lisa Curry and international businesswomen, philanthropists, health warriors and women whose personal lives are inspirational in their own right.

It was a feat, with forty-two interviews generating more than 200,000 words of content, which I then whittled down to 24,000 words, cementing the most impactful versions of each woman's story. The launch event was a true celebration of the fighting spirit we have inside all of us.

Narrative nonfiction

This is where you can have a blend! You can, for example, combine a self-help book with a memoir. You may recognise this as the format I utilised when working with Unstoppable Force CEO and founder Stew Darling, a former Lieutenant Colonel in Military Intelligence with a twenty-three-year career in the British Army running security, intelligence, and counter-intelligence operations around the world.

Since launching *Lead through Life*, Stew has applied his extensive skills and experience to make a difference in the lives of individuals and businesses. I discussed this book in *The Mindful Author* when highlighting the potential for people to transform both personally and professionally when they write their books.

We were able to combine Stew's decades of leadership experience, the practical knowledge he gained, and his personal life with the framework he developed. This powerful narrative ensured that his life story became the thread that highlighted the impact of his framework and showed the reader how it came to be developed. It was not something he simply dreamed up one day – each and every step could be linked to a poignant moment in his life.

This boosted the educational impact of the book immensely because people learn through stories. With the lessons becoming more relevant to the readers, Stew was able to connect with them, and they went on to buy his second book, *Unstoppable Force*, secure him for speaking or presentations at large events or sign up to become coaching clients.

We will cover some structures to present narrative nonfiction in the upcoming Structure chapter, but for now, I'd love to introduce you to a different way of thinking about your story.

10 story types

The mastermind behind the Disney film *Blank Check* and the author of the *Save the Cat* trilogy, the late Blake Snyder, was renowned for his view on how to create screenplays that captivated audiences. He coined the title of his series to describe a decisive moment in every story when the protagonist demonstrates that they are worth supporting in their quest, whatever that may be. Like me, Snyder was a stickler for structure and his books continue to show aspiring screenwriters how to plan out their scripts with essential story 'beats'.

Just as I have explained the nonfiction subgenres in order to give you a greater understanding of how your story fits into the grand scheme of the nonfiction world, Snyder also introduced ten story types in his book that distinguished the content and feel of the protagonist's story arc depending on genre. Snyder believed that traditional genres such as romantic comedy, epic or biography are not descriptive enough of the story itself, merely serving to describe the movie genre.

Nonfiction subgenres

Snyder's system of 10 story types explores genre in-depth and many of the same principles of storytelling apply within nonfiction works. Having knowledge and an understanding of Snyder's concepts and 10 story types can help you formulate your own approach.

Here, I walk you through the 10 story types and share a book and author that fits each category. These titles all sit on my own writing-cave shelf. The majority are written by everyday people, not celebrities.

Hopefully, you can see just how easy it is for your story to be just as powerful as a Hollywood blockbuster plot!

1. Monster in the house

These take us to our most primal instincts. The story usually centres around a protagonist who is trapped with a monster in a defined setting. The setting or 'house' can be anything as long as it is inescapable. The monster is typically a metaphor. An act of sin invites the monster into the setting, and it is only after the sin is acknowledged and atoned for that the monster can be destroyed.

Example: Janelle Parson's *House of Shadows*. House of Shadows is a powerful, inspiring memoir of one woman's journey to achieve what most would think impossible. Growing up in a household with an abusive father, Janelle grows into a young woman who seeks the comfort of the familiar –
a partner who is also abusive. The monster, in this context, is

intergenerational abuse and Janelle, as the protagonist, sets off to break free of the grips of the vicious cycle in order to free herself, her children and future generations of their family.

2. Golden fleece

This is a journey or quest. Golden fleece stories usually have a prize or goal that the main character needs to obtain or achieve in a timeframe. The protagonist often assembles a team along the way to achieve this goal or obtain the prize. The joy of this style of story is in the journey, not in reaching the destination.

Example: Kellie Harriden's *Long-Awaited Child* is the true story of an Australian woman who travels across continents to beat the odds in order to fulfil her quest to be a mother. Strength and resilience, hope and perseverance; this book provides a deeply personal insight into the often-unspoken challenges of infertility.

3. Out of the bottle

These are parables about people appreciating what they have and making the necessary changes to maintain the things they treasure. Typically, this storyline involves a character who is either successful or struggling with their situation, a wish is expressed and a spell or plot device is introduced that takes the protagonist and places them in circumstances that are the opposite of their current existence. The audience enjoys witnessing the protagonist navigate the new world, and eventually, the protagonist realises that the skills developed in their previous situation are what make them special. The protagonist learns a lesson and returns to their previous existence, armed with new knowledge and confidence for the road ahead.

Example: Angie Mansey's *How I Made Lemonade*. This is no highlight reel. Angie's inspirational story shows how she put the pieces back together after heartbreaking divorces and enduring a devastating miscarriage before becoming a devoted carer for her medically complex son  through more than twenty surgeries. This story of hope shows the power of never giving up and the importance of defiantly moving forward.

4. Buddy love

These are stories about human beings who find love and purpose in their relationships with others. The plotline can revolve around various types of relationships, including friendships, romantic love, pets or even robots! The story begins with a protagonist who is incomplete yet does not realise something is missing from their life. Then, a counterpart is introduced who is often the antithesis of the protagonist and carries the missing component that will make the protagonist complete. The two often clash but slowly discover each other's strengths. A complication is introduced that tears the team apart, but they ultimately reform, and each borrows lessons from the other.

Example: Angela Williams' *Extravagant Life to Extravagant Love*. Entering the red-light areas of England's most violent cities is not somewhere people usually dream of venturing. However, for Angela, this became her reality. Born into one of the wealthiest families in England and the  daughter of a British lord, Angela journeys between ballgowns to boots to give readers an intimate, honest and somewhat humorous behind-the-scenes look into the dichotomies of living between two opposite worlds. Her commitment to show extravagant love not only changes their lives but hers too. This book is a challenging and powerful reminder that we each have a divine purpose: to love humankind just as Jesus did – with extravagance.

5. Whydunit

Snyder believed 'why' is always more compelling than 'who' when it comes to mystery stories. In a whydunit story, the protagonist does not need to be a detective, but they will still perform that role as they collect and decipher clues and use their knowledge to solve the mystery. The dark turn is the point where the hunt for truth leaves the protagonist unsafe, whether or not the truth is revealed.

Example: Alex Gerrick's *A Season of Clouds*. To his friends, family and work colleagues, Alex is a successful senior bureaucrat, well respected and liked by those who view him as an inspirational leader. But behind the facade, Alex is tormented by his past traumas, especially his betrayal of a young

woman while on holiday in Greece in 1995. As Alex's mental health begins to deteriorate rapidly, he realises that his life has mostly been a lie and that the key to his immediate survival rests with several people he briefly met when he was a younger man. Can Alex use their belated wisdom to defeat his inner demons before he reaches the point of no return?

6. Dude with a problem

'Human with a problem' stories refer to narratives where the protagonist is unexpectedly forced, while going about their daily life, to confront a conflict that puts them in a life-or-death situation. This conflict forces the protagonist to take action and face the situation head-on.

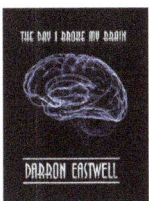

Example: Darron Eastwell's *The Day I Broke My Brain*. In May of 2015, successful banking executive Darron Eastwell had plans for an exciting day of mountain biking at Tewantin National Park. No one could have known that the day would end with Darron lying in a coma, his future uncertain. Darron emerged from that experience as a brain injury survivor. *The Day I Broke My Brain* is a true story of overcoming the most difficult of circumstances with courage, perseverance, and a dash of humour.

7. Institutionalised

These stories centre around an individual's battle with a society, group or institution. There is often a group that the protagonist belongs to, and through an event, or series of events, the character is forced into a world where they have to make a choice to confront either an opposite society/institution/group or their own society/institution/group.

Example: Jodie Nolan's *Surviving the Storm*. *Surviving the Storm* takes readers on a journey of how one woman overcame despair and desperation to claim back her life and her millions. Ready to retire at thirty, Jodie was in hospital giving birth to her first baby when the storm hit. It offers a rare insight into how a successful career in finance turned suddenly to destroy everything she worked for and the impact it had on many Australian families like Jodie's. Written from the perspective of a woman, mother and leading Australian financial adviser with more than fifteen years' experience, *Surviving the Storm* shares tips that financial advisors don't want customers to know and strategies that the everyday person can easily implement to benefit their financial future.

8. Fool triumphant

This protagonist is unaware of any greatness they may possess. The fool enters a world, establishment, or institution and, due to their lack of awareness, causes conflict. Others may try with all their might to destroy the fool, but the fool narrowly escapes each attempt through luck and happenstance. Eventually, the fool becomes aware and is able to mutate into a hero and bring down the establishment to create positive change.

Nonfiction subgenres

Example: Flea's *Acid for the Children*. There is no ill-will intended with this book selection, but I felt the way in which Flea showcases how he was pushed down multiple times on his rise to the heights of rock 'n' roll fame was a great fit for this story type.  The strange tale of a boy named Flea starts in Rye, NY. It was all very normal. But soon his parents divorced and his mother Patricia remarried a jazz musician. Flea's stepfather frequently invited musicians to his house for jam sessions which sparked Flea's interest in music. The family moved to Los Angeles, where Flea became fascinated with the trumpet, idolising musicians like Miles, Dizzy, and Louis. But the family soon fell apart. He began smoking weed at thirteen and became a daily user of harder drugs. He was on the streets by fourteen and soon after, met another social outcast and drug user named Anthony Kiedis. They formed a band that would become the Red Hot Chili Peppers.

9. Rites of passage

This is usually centred around internal conflict. The protagonist is confronted with a life problem that upends their normal existence and sends them on a path of self-discovery. The protagonist spends much of the story dealing with and confronting the problem in counterproductive and damaging ways. Finally, the protagonist realises that only through acceptance can a new life or existence begin.

Example: Carren Smith's *Soul Survivor*. In 2001, Carren Smith's partner committed suicide. Immediately, she was catapulted into the depths of darkness and despair. Carrying enormous guilt, responsibility and self-hatred for the next twelve months, Carren began to think the only way out was taking her own life. Almost to the date, twelve months later, the world was rocked as terrorists struck the heart of humanity once again in the 2002 Bali Bombings. Trapped by bodies, limbs and the call of death, Carren found herself in a fight for survival that was driven only by human instinct and the heat of the fire at her feet.

10. Superhero

This is not always about beings with magical abilities but rather focuses on the burden of possessing talents. The protagonist is endowed with a special power that is both a blessing and a curse because it is a barrier between the hero and society. A nemesis is introduced who is ruthless in the pursuit of their own goal and knows that the hero is a threat. The hero must make a choice to accept the power as a blessing and willingly accept the burden of the curse to defeat the nemesis.

Example: An interesting fit of the superhero category is Jake LaMotta's *Raging Bull: My story*. Meet Jake LaMotta – thief, rapist, killer. Raised in the Bronx slums, he fought on the streets, got sent to reform school, and served time in prison. Trusting no one, slugging everyone, he beat his wife, his best friends, and even the mobsters who kept the title just out of reach. Those same forces that made him a criminal – fear, rage, jealousy, self-hate, guilt – combined with his drive and intelligence made him a winner in the ring. At age twenty-seven, after eight years of fighting, he became the world middleweight champion, a hero to thousands. Then, at the peak of success, he fell apart and began a swift, harrowing descent into a nightmare. *Raging Bull*, the Bronx Bull's brutally candid memoir, tells it all – fights, jails, sex, money – surpassing, in hard-hitting prose, even the movie that immortalised it.

MAP IT OUT

Now that you have discovered the different subgenres, where do you think your book fits? Is it a single category or a combination that you are going to draw from in order to make a narrative nonfiction?

Head back to your mind map and add in any further thoughts you have had since learning about the subgenres. They could include:

- new topics
- stories or knowledge that links in with a specific theme
- beliefs and points that are vital to showing who you are.

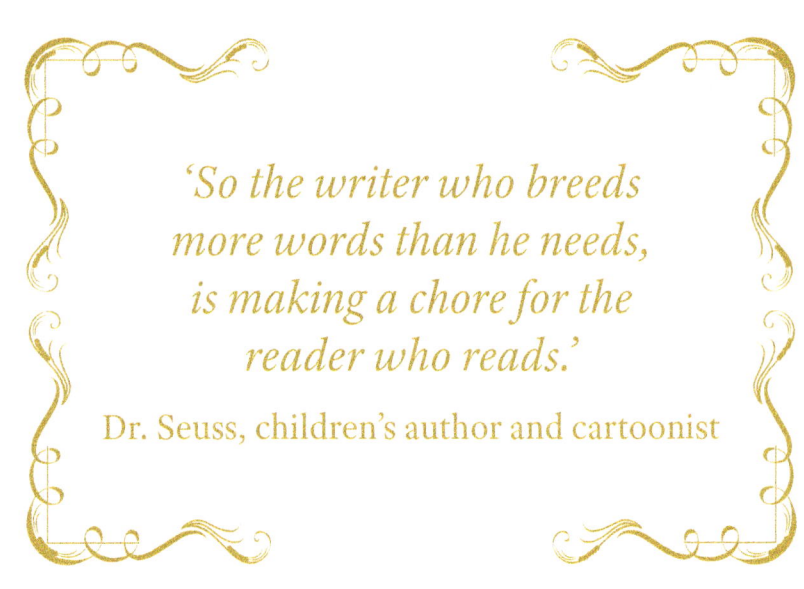

'So the writer who breeds more words than he needs, is making a chore for the reader who reads.'

Dr. Seuss, children's author and cartoonist

Structure

This is where we arrive at the juicy part of structuring your book – deciding on the flow that you would like to engage. Again, there are many, many ways in which you can present your story. Some of them are tried and tested with definite formulas, others are a little less rigid and offer those who desire flexibility to soar.

I am a firm believer that creativity is subjective. You can never say there is only one path forward for authors to create a powerful structure. It's true, though, that you don't have to necessarily reinvent the wheel. It's important to learn from those who have come before and see what you are drawn to and what you find an utter bore. Sometimes, knowing what you don't like is more powerful than knowing what you do.

In this case, knowledge is power, so this chapter is dedicated to showing you some of the most popular ways to structure nonfiction books. Read through each of them, and as you go, reflect on which feels like a good fit for your style of story. You will be able to exclude some structure types immediately; you can keep others in mind to mull over. You may be fortunate enough to read one of the following structure ideas and see your story already start to unfold within that frame. If you do, don't question it! Follow your intuition and let it guide you.

Chronological

Chronology – presenting things in order – makes perfect sense for a how-to or self-help book, as these subgenres rely on building layers of knowledge. You have to start at step one and

Structure

make your way through to the final step in order to complete the journey, learn the skill or master the process.

But the trouble with applying this to a memoir or autobiography is that telling a lifetime of stories in order means you could be selling your story short. So many people have a compulsion to start with some variation of, 'I was born on a cold winter's night, August 18, 1968...'

Yawn! Unless your birth was some sort of miracle, it rarely warrants being the first thing the reader learns about you.

Seem strange? Let me put it this way: the most compelling books – fiction or nonfiction – usually set out to solve some sort of problem; it may be a problem for the reader, such as how to make a million dollars or a child's development from baby to preschool, or it may be to show your reader how you faced a problem and overcame it.

If your story falls into the latter category, finding ways to really bring home what that problem is in the first few paragraphs is going to be the difference between a page-turner and a humdrum reading experience.

There is a caveat here: writing things in the order that they happened can be a great way to help you organise a memoir or autobiography because it takes the confusion out of the storytelling flow if writing is new to you. It allows you to get everything down onto the page for your first draft, *but* please don't think it's always the best way to present your story to your final reader.

Traditional three acts

This is as easy as it gets in terms of structure – there's a beginning, a middle and an end.

The beginning is where you set the scene, introduce the main characters (you and the people who are featuring in your story) and depict how things were before the major problem arises.

In the middle, the antagonist comes into play. It doesn't have to be a stereotypical human villain; the antagonist could be a disease, a financial situation, a natural disaster, or anything out of the ordinary that causes tension and threatens to change the life of the main character/s the reader now knows.

The end portion is where the characters face off against the antagonist and the conflict reaches its peak before the resolution. You may choose to leave the reader with the victory or continue on to give more context of what life is like post-conflict and how the character/s have evolved as a result of the journey.

The drop-in

Love books that smack you in the face as soon as you start reading? There's nothing I love more than manipulating time in books. With the drop-in, you can start your story at *any* point along the chronology and then cycle back to the beginning to build context and begin the journey.

Excitement bubbles in me when I think about all of the possibilities that come when you choose a drop-in structure!

Structure

You could choose to start at the end when the antagonist has been subdued and the main character is living a life they never thought possible. You could drop the reader into the middle of the conflict with the antagonist and show the battle in full-blown action. You could choose to select a moment in time when the main character was faced with a choice, a metaphorical fork in the road and the decision could be the difference between life or death.

Drop-ins are most effective when you choose a moment that is emotionally charged. I mean any emotion. It doesn't have to be anger, sadness, fear or anxiety-inducing; it can be something shocking, unexpected, joyful or even hilarious.

If you can engage some sort of emotional response from your reader in the first chapter, you know you have chosen a winner.

Your drop-in may be 100 per cent clear as you read this, or you may have several possible drop-in points to choose from. To save you from getting stuck in limbo waiting for 'the one' to rise to the surface in your lake of possibilities, start writing your first draft chronologically, and you can always do a slight reshuffle of content once you settle on the most impactful drop-in.

From experience, I find 'the one' will make itself clear as you begin writing. There will be something that triggers a response in you: tears, heat rising from anger, an involuntary chuckle or maybe even goosebumps. As soon as you experience any of those, your intuition is helping to guide you to appreciate the power of that experience.

Parallel

Parallel structures are popular in movie scripts and fiction because they allow two different storylines to unfold in unison. Novelists like Dan Brown will give readers the perspective of the hero and the antagonist, each taking turns to advance their journeys until they eventually cross paths and the storylines merge into the book's climax – the conflict.

A structure like this can work in nonfiction, but it requires two compelling storylines with a common thread to make it work. A co-authored book allows two different perspectives on the same event, such as mother and son Jane and Zac Jones' *Why the Fallen?* The authors shares how they independently navigated Zac's imprisonment. Their relationship was pushed beyond the limits, and then Zac found his redemption behind bars while his mother rediscovered her son in prison.

In *The Immortal Life of Henrietta Lacks*, author Rebecca Skloot tells the story of a woman whose cancer cells were taken without her knowledge and used for scientific research. By utilising a parallel structure, Skloot is able to alternate between Henrietta's experience and the scientific discoveries that were made using the harvested cells.

The hero's journey

The hero's journey is the template on which many successful movies, such as *Star Wars* and *The Wizard of Oz*, are based. Is it a process that provides a path so well-worn that you can plot

Structure

most Hollywood blockbusters off it (which unfortunately has the potential to lead to predictability, so be careful!)

This most widely used character arc for a traditional writing structure began to take shape in Joseph Campbell's *The Hero with a Thousand Faces*.[4] It became popularised and was further refined by Hollywood development executive, screenwriter and author Christopher Vogler in his Twelve Stage Hero's Journey.[5]

Each step has a very thorough explanation of what it should entail in order to maximise the story arc – or journey – of the main character. In a nutshell, you set the scene for what your ordinary life is before a major antagonist challenges that way of life. The reader is then taken on that journey of self-belief, self-discovery and ultimately, the conflict with the antagonist.

Often, success is not won in the first conflict, and there may be several setbacks after which the main character may question their ability to defeat the antagonist. But then, some sort of power is bestowed upon the main character – a pearl of wisdom, physical weapon or mystical knowledge – that equips them with what they need to finally emerge victorious.

Thus, life resumes, but it is not the same life as the one the main character started with, because the journey has changed them forever.

The twelve stages of the Hero's Journey

1. Ordinary world
   Your ordinary life is on display, and the readers get to know who you are so they can connect with you as the story progresses.

2. Call to adventure
   The 'adventure' begins, and it disrupts the ordinary world.

3. Refusal of the call
   This is where the fears of the hero come into play. They may have doubts about whether they can make the changes they need to and face the demons that are knocking on the metaphorical door or step up and be brave enough to face the change that is afoot.

4. Meeting the mentor
   Everyone needs guidance, and this is where we meet the mentor who equips the hero with the knowledge and/or skills to face the adventure.

5. Crossing the threshold
   The hero now starts to take action, either willingly or because they are forced.

6. Tests, allies, enemies
   The hero is confronted by more challenges that test body, mind and spirit. All of this happens as the

hero has to learn who to trust and navigate their path through the various hurdles on the way to the end goal.

7. Approach to the inmost cave

    The inmost cave doesn't have to be a physical location. It may represent an inner conflict which, up until now, the hero has not had to face. At the threshold to the inmost cave, the hero may once again face some of the doubts and fears that first surfaced upon the call to adventure.

8. Ordeal

    The supreme ordeal may be a dangerous physical test or a deep inner crisis that the hero must face in order to survive, or for the world in which the hero lives to continue to exist. Only through some form of 'death' can the hero be reborn. Again, this doesn't have to be literal. It can be a decision to leave something behind, to accept something as it is, to forgive. This gives the hero the power to reach the end goal.

9. Reward (seizing the sword)

    After defeating the supreme ordeal, the hero is ultimately transformed into a new state, emerging from battle as a stronger person and often with a prize. The reward could be a new 'power', a secret, more wisdom or repairing damage to a relationship with another or themselves. But the story is not yet over.

10. The road back

    The hero returns home with the reward, but there may be one last pushback on the way to the ordinary world.

11. Resurrection

    The final battle represents something far greater than the hero's own existence; the outcome of this final challenge will impact everyone. If the hero fails, others will suffer; if the hero wins, everything will start afresh.

12. Return with the elixir

    This is the final stage of the journey in which the hero returns to the ordinary world as a changed person. There has been personal growth, new wisdom gained and fresh hope for all. While the return is often physically to where the hero started, the hero's experiences mean they will never be the same again.

Please exercise caution when looking at the hero's journey for your structure. It works well for screenwriting and fiction because you can create events that fit the mould. As you know, real-life never unfolds according to a predictable formula. Remember the concept of accidental inauthenticity I shared in *The Mindful Author*? There is potential for you to venture into that territory if you start to shift the timelines of your life story in order to fit this structure.

Structure

My advice is to use the hero's journey formula as inspiration rather than an immovable blueprint. You can still see how you evolved through the challenge you were faced with and use the twelve steps as markers to make sure you cover all of the elements of your story, but if you came up against many more challenges than just two or three, build them into your own unique journey. After all, every hero has their own superpower, so make sure you stay true to revealing what yours is.

Self-contained

If your book covers a subject with many individual sections that won't run together in a narrative, you can structure your book by topics. This provides you with nice little containers to place your content into, which will focus your writing.

You can view the self-contained structure as though you are a teacher or coach, giving your student – the reader – everything they need. Even though this is a more prescriptive way of structuring a book, you can still harness the power of stories. In fact, I encourage storytelling in every style of book because people are more likely to remember new things in the context of a story. For how-to structures, your stories can be based on successes to emulate or fails to avoid. In self-help styles, you can include case studies for people you have worked with or for.

Listicles also fall into the self-contained realm, as each point is its own entity. Everything you need to know about that tip needs to be included in that list item.

Let's look at Ignite & Write Mentorship alum Dr Judy McHugh as a great example. Judy had completed a PhD and published a thesis on domestic violence in the 1990s. Throughout her professional career, she worked as a counsellor and used her knowledge of abusive relationships to teach women how to recognise the signs of abuse and how to rebuild satisfying lives free of abuse. Judy wanted to write a book that presented updated information from her thesis so it would appeal to the everyday person. She wanted to remove the academic speak and replace it with real-life events and situations that women have found themselves in.

When it came to creating a structure for Judy, we found a topic approach to be the most appropriate. She could then identify individual stages of the cycle of abuse and focus on them individually in each chapter, explaining what the behaviour looks like, how it presents in different relationships and give examples from women who have experienced it. This gave her the freedom to explore each stage in-depth and give the reader many opportunities to connect with the reported actions, words and behaviours of other domestic violence abusers to see if they were being mirrored in their own homes.

Another book that written using this topic approach is the parent guide, *Sexts, Texts & Selfies*, by Susan McLean. The information, aimed at parents of teens, is broken down into sections on creating good online habits, digital reputation, defining an online friend, cyberbullying, nudes and naked selfies, gaming habits, supportive tips and resources.

When it comes to penning your own book, you can choose to treat each topic as its own 'mini book' with a beginning, middle and end. Alternatively, you might prefer to create more of a thread that connects one chapter to the next. The latter can be

Structure

as simple as briefly introducing what the next step or topic is and why it's important to the overall knowledge you are sharing.

Collaborative or co-authored books always treat each chapter as its own self-contained story. Most collaborative books will have a common theme that the stories are linked to, but with each chapter being written by a different person, they are more like a collection of short stories.

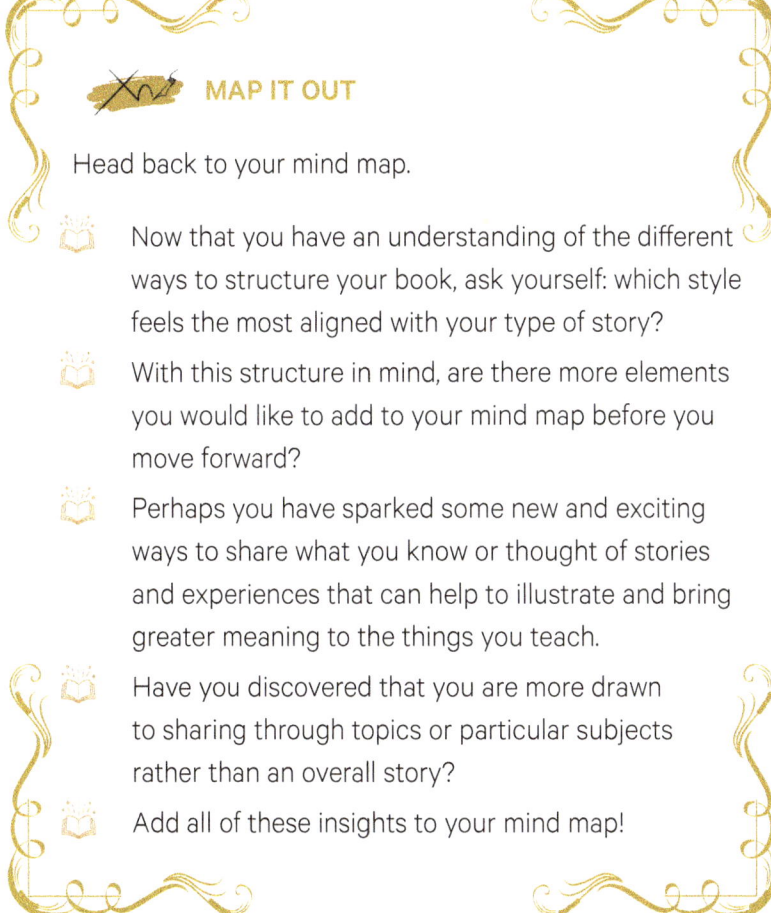

MAP IT OUT

Head back to your mind map.

- Now that you have an understanding of the different ways to structure your book, ask yourself: which style feels the most aligned with your type of story?
- With this structure in mind, are there more elements you would like to add to your mind map before you move forward?
- Perhaps you have sparked some new and exciting ways to share what you know or thought of stories and experiences that can help to illustrate and bring greater meaning to the things you teach.
- Have you discovered that you are more drawn to sharing through topics or particular subjects rather than an overall story?
- Add all of these insights to your mind map!

> *'It's kind of fun to do the impossible.'*
>
> Walt Disney, animator, film producer and entrepreneur

Creating your manuscript structure

With all of your key points and major structure components laid out on your mind map, you've done all of the legwork. Now it's time to pull it together into a structure.

While you were reading through the types of nonfiction books and the structures for each of them, was there one that stood out? One that you feel would allow you to communicate your style of story best?

Keep that in mind as you sit in front of your mind map. It's time! Everything you have been working towards so far is about to pay dividends. I recommend that you allow yourself a block of uninterrupted time for this next step, as your mind will be firing on all cylinders, connecting dots and possibly even seeing the story begin to unfold.

The creative experience is different for each person, so don't worry if you encounter something completely different when pulling your mind map into a structure; there is no right or wrong.

 **MAP IT OUT**

All you need to begin this transformation is your mind map, a plain old boring lead pencil and an eraser. We move away from anything 'permanent' in this step so you can leave perfectionism and the compulsion to 'get it right' in the cupboard. Remain in that free, creative space and know that things will shift and move around as you work through this process. You can absolutely

Creating your manuscript structure

erase the markings you make in this step three, five, maybe even ten times until you feel complete. It's all totally okay!

I will now take you through step-by-step instructions on how to create your manuscript structure.

1. Grab your finished mind map, pencil and eraser and ensure you will be uninterrupted for a solid block of time. I recommend at least twenty minutes.

2. Think about the nonfiction subgenre you feel best suits your story. If you haven't already, write it on your mind map with your pencil.

3. Turn your attention to the different structure styles from the previous chapter. Which feels the most aligned with your story?

4. Now is the time for action. With the structure you've chosen in mind, grab your pencil and look at the branches on your mind map. Are there some elements that could be grouped together?

    For example, is there something you teach that was the result of something you lived? Were there several life events that unfolded in unison or so intertwined that you could not possibly separate them? Give each group its own shape or symbol. I use basic shapes like circles, squares, triangles, rectangles, stars. If there are so many groups that I run out of shapes, I'll assign a circle with dots in it or a circle with a squiggle in the middle to ensure each group has its own unique identification.

There may not be any groups at all, and that's okay. Don't force things to link together if it is not immediately apparent to you.

5. Now that you have your groups, switch to numbers. That's right, you need to be brave now and allocate each branch or group its own number. This number will be the order you would like it to appear in your book. If you are going with a self-contained style of book, think about the order in which readers may need to know each topic. If this is important, it will guide your chapter order. If it is not, you can play around with the order and see how it feels.

If you have chosen more of a narrative style and you aren't clear on what your drop-in might be, stick with creating chronological flow. This will free you from the burden of making a decision now. When you reach your second draft stage, you will likely be clear on the event or situation where you'd like to start your reader. Then all you require is a little content shuffle.

If you have already had the pleasure of the drop-in point illuminating in your mind as clear as day, place a huge one next to it! You would usually then come back to chronological order to move through the rest of the book, so number the branches or groups accordingly.

Creating your manuscript structure

6. Continue step five until all of your major branches or groups have a number assigned to them. The order may change as you go through this, so do not allow frustration to creep in – it's rare to nail this on the first attempt. Your story will start to unfold as you move through this. Consecutive elements you thought made sense at the start may need to be moved as you move further through this process. Just erase, reassign the numbers and keep going.

7. Once everything is numbered, sit back and marvel at your handiwork!

8. Head to a computer, laptop or whatever device you prefer to write longform on, and create the document for your structure. This is where your mind map becomes a list. Type up your chapters in order, with a bold heading followed by any associated notes from its group. These points will help to guide the content of your chapter once you get writing.

9. Create headings in your document. These are clickable links that help you to navigate easily to different chapters without having to mindlessly scroll as your word count climbs. This feature is available in most word-processing software, so you don't have to go searching for anything fancy to achieve this.

    Take the humble Microsoft Word, for example, make sure the Home tab is selected. In the Styles window, you will see Heading 1, 2, 3 etc. Heading 1 is a main chapter heading, while 2 and 3 can be used as subheadings within a chapter.

Alternatively, you can download my Manuscript Template from the Ignite & Write Resource Centre here:

You can then personalise it with your own working chapter titles. You don't have to lock in the final chapter names at this early stage, so use anything as a placeholder that will help you remember the content you intend to place in each chapter.

You've completed your manuscript structure! Celebrate!

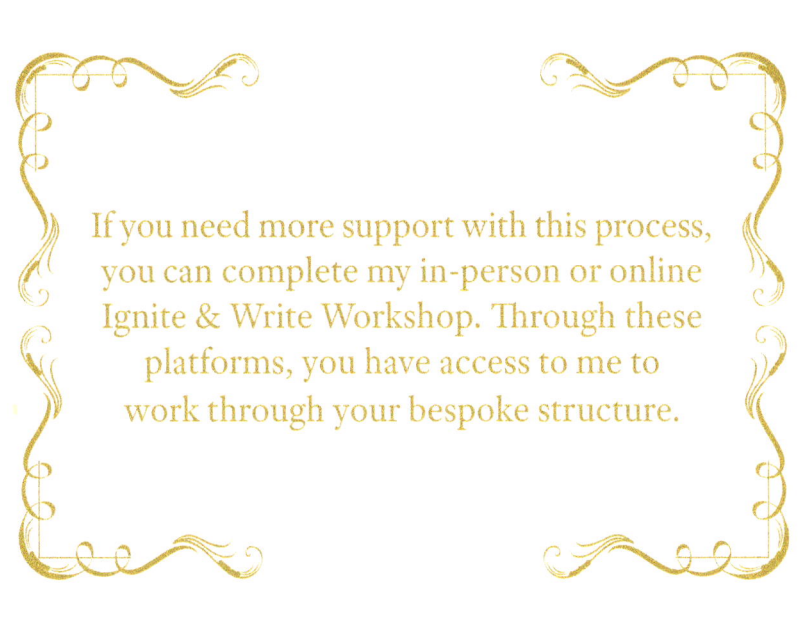

If you need more support with this process, you can complete my in-person or online Ignite & Write Workshop. Through these platforms, you have access to me to work through your bespoke structure.

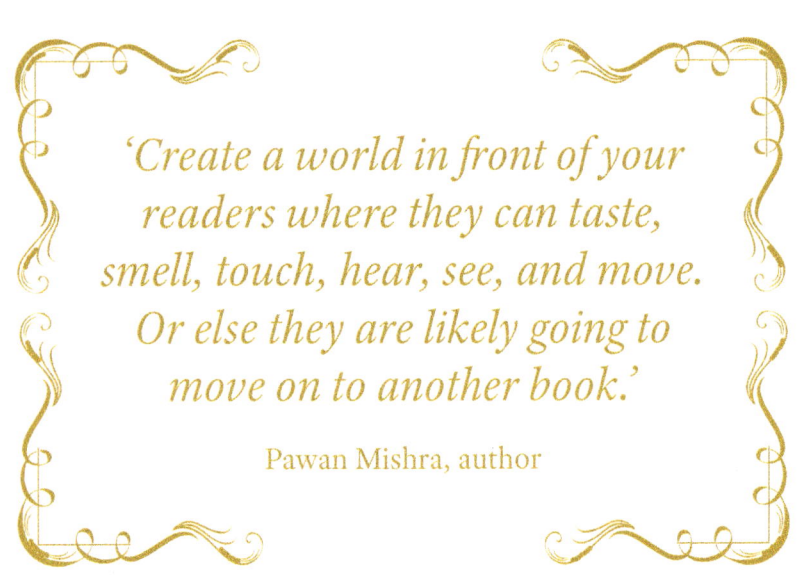

'Create a world in front of your readers where they can taste, smell, touch, hear, see, and move. Or else they are likely going to move on to another book.'

Pawan Mishra, author

Chapter structure

Now that your overall manuscript structure is in place, we can focus on the structure of each chapter. Whether it is a self-contained chapter that has its own mini-journey to share or the reader is strapping in from page one and following your narrative all the way to the end of the book, it is important to understand how people consume content so you can make sure you are catering to all kinds of readers.

Luckily for us, the amazing minds at Harvard University have taken the guesswork out of what that looks like.[6] There are three types of readers:

- Cerebral readers need context. They need to know *why* something is important to them before they are prepared to invest their time, in this case, to read the chapters.
- Emotional learners crave the journey and storytelling. They want to know *how* everything happened, to be taken by the hand and to be guided through the book.
- Impatient fact finders don't care about the why or the how; they just want to know *what* to do.

Although they are all looking for different things from their experience of your book, there are simple ways you can cater to all three types of readers, no matter what subgenre or structure you have chosen.

Make sure you start off the chapter to engage the cerebral readers. For self-contained styles, this will include great hints for your reader about why this chapter exists and why it is

Chapter structure

important to the book. For narrative styles, launching into a scene and creating context will allow cerebral readers to engage in the *why* and settle in for the next instalment of your story. (If you have used a cliffhanger to end the previous chapter, the work would have been done for you already 😉)

The largest chunk of each chapter – the 75 per cent in the middle – is for the emotional learners. No matter what structure you have chosen, this middle section is where you take the reader on the journey. For education-style books, you are showing *how* to do the thing. For narrative-style books, you are showing the reader *how* you navigated this stage of your story.

Impatient fact finders (IFF) are often forgotten for the simple reason that most of us who take the time to pour our heart and soul into a book expect that everyone who picks it up is going to read it from cover to cover. *Gasp!* This is simply not the case.

I met a real-life IFF once. I was working alongside her in the Ignite & Write Mentorship program, guiding her through writing her first draft. When I shared the three reader styles, she piped up with, 'Oh yeah, that's me! I once went into a bookstore and picked up the book I wanted to read and saw the table of contents had listed out all the steps, so I got everything I needed just from that!'

Once I picked my jaw up off the floor, I remembered even those who only wish to get in, get out, and get on with it still need to be factored in when writing your book. For self-contained and educational-style books, any of the following elements will help to engage the IFFs:

- a chapter summary that could be placed into a box or written in a different font
- key takeaways, literal bullet points that convey the most important elements of the chapter
- actionable steps, things for the reader to *do*.

These can be harder to include in narrative books because it breaks the flow of the story. Do not fear! The way to capture IFFs, if you have chosen a narrative style, is to use pull quotes, which you would have already noted among these pages. Pull quotes are essentially sentences that you feel are impactful enough to warrant being given a larger font, maybe even a different colour, to draw the reader's eye to them.

> By being selective with which sentences you choose, you can create a journey for those who skim through the book, allowing them to take in the points that you value the most.

When it comes to the number of chapters and how long they 'need' to be, there really are no hard and fast rules. If your structure is topic-based, you will already know the number of chapters that are necessary to cover your chosen themes, so this takes the guesswork out of it for you!

For narrative styles, I have seen some books that are divided into five lengthy, in-depth chapters. Others, like Prince Harry's

Chapter structure

memoir *Spare*, dedicate a chapter to each short anecdote or theme. As a result, his book is made up of 232 chapters spread across three parts. Ultimately, it comes back to how you would like your ideal reader to navigate your book.

You may be tempted to overcrowd your chapters with multiple ideas in order to share as much as you can, but you will quickly realise that often less is more. When you spread out your story or teachings across a couple of chapters instead of cramming multiple ideas into one, you can go into greater depth on each subject or situation and enhance your reader's experience.

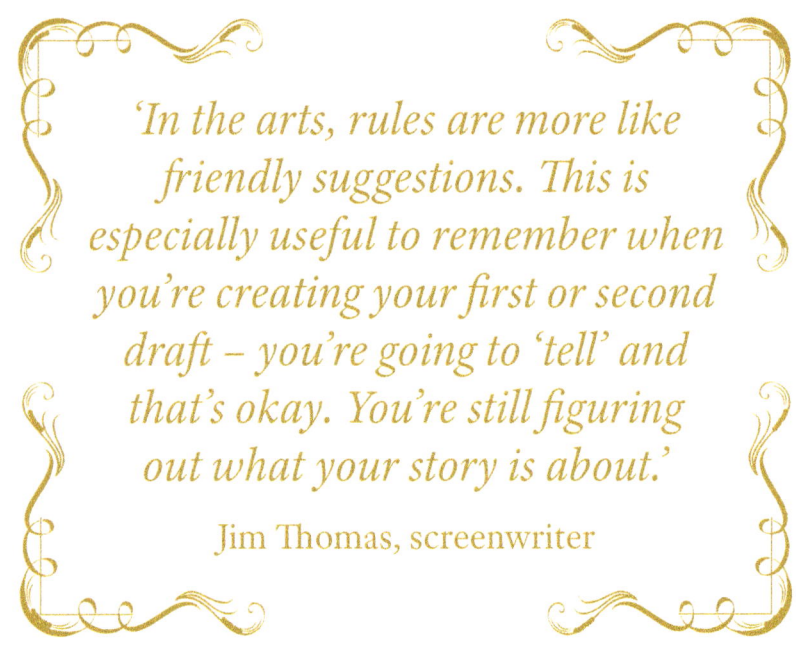

'In the arts, rules are more like friendly suggestions. This is especially useful to remember when you're creating your first or second draft – you're going to 'tell' and that's okay. You're still figuring out what your story is about.'

Jim Thomas, screenwriter

Writing

Ignite & Write: *The Structured Author*

In his book *On Writing*, the great international bestselling novelist Stephen King – you may have heard of him... he's published 63 novels and 200 short stories – says all you need to become a writer is to read and write. You can do that. So, you actually have everything you need. I would, however, add a third requisite to King's requirements. To become an author, and not just a writer, you need a *structure*. Guess what? You now have that up your sleeve, too!

The time you have spent laying the strong foundations for your book will pay dividends as you embark on the next phase of your book creation – writing! As you know, people who skip all of the steps before this and jump in with excitement to create content may not have a pleasant experience all the way through.

You know *what* you are writing, *why* you are writing it, *who* you are writing for and *how* you are going to write it. There is nothing more beautiful than clarity when it comes to capturing a lifetime of memories and experience, and you now have that in spades.

One of the other beautiful things about having your structure in place is that you have freed yourself from the burden of having to write your book from start to end. The chapter headings in your manuscript document allow you to navigate to any area of your book where you feel called to write. I encourage you to do that!

Far too often, I see people stuck in the mud because they can't get the first paragraph, first page or first chapter out. They are overwhelmed about making the right sort of impact straight out of the gate.

Give yourself grace. This may be the first time you dedicate some serious time to writing, so let me share a piece of wisdom that will take a huge burden off your shoulders: nobody, I repeat nobody, publishes their first draft. In fact, nobody even has to see a single page of it.

There is a technical term for the first step in the writing process, and it's called the Shitty First Draft (SFD) or a Barf Draft. I'm not even joking. SFD is commonly used because even the finest modern literary greats – even Stephen King himself – cannot punch out a print-worthy, error-free manuscript on the first attempt.

The end result that you buy from bookstores and online platforms has gone through many evolutions, from the SFD to the second, third, and maybe even fourth draft, as the book runs through editing, proofing and formatting. Each stage catches more typos, corrects grammatical errors and tightens up sentences.

Trying to do all of this and more while writing your first draft is going to turn what could be a fun, creative and rewarding process into a nail-biting, hair-raising nightmare. Not only that, but you will feel like your manuscript is in a perpetual Groundhog Day because you are working and reworking the same page (or even paragraph) on repeat.

> Don't try to be perfect in
> the first instance.

Free yourself to be in the moment of creation. Leave the self-judgement at the door and pour everything that has been buzzing around your head onto those pages. Your pre-created structure will ensure there is order around how and where you place your thoughts. This places you leagues ahead of those who simply sit down and write with no planning, preparation or purpose.

Remember, writing a book is a new skill.

It might appear easy, but it is common to underestimate the writing process. There will be tough days, and at times, it might feel like it's taking forever, and you start to question why you signed up for this in the first place. But trust me, it is well worth it if you hang in there.

You are not a professional writer; that is why you have this book in your hands. You need support and guidance to show you the way. Congratulate yourself for seeking out that help rather than feeling like you have to slog your way through on your own.

This section will guide you through writing your SFD and revising and editing to create a second draft. (Heads up! Book Three of the *Ignite & Write Trilogy*, *The Published Author*, will walk you through the rest of the steps required in order to hold that physical book in your hand.)

The journey of a thousand miles begins with the first step, so know that it will take a few shaky steps at first to build confidence in your writing muscle so you can progress with more ease.

You've got this, and I've got you.

Tapping into your creativity

Creativity is something we innately have. That's right, we are born creative! Somewhere along the way, we 'grow up', and the obligations of life take over. Of course, some lucky souls remain connected to their inner child, the place where imagination and creativity still roam free.

I'll be the first to admit that I am the biggest child at heart. On a 2024 trip to Legoland in Japan, I was bouncing up and down with excitement as we stood in front of the massive Lego façade entry gate while my kids inched away from me in embarrassment and my husband rolled his eyes.

Even if you feel like life has worn you down, there is an inner creative buried deep within that is just waiting to be unleashed. All you need to do is give this energy permission to come to the fore. To help you along, here are my top tips for helping you to get in touch with your creativity:

Self-identify as an author – now

As you know, it is so important to keep your mindset in check while writing your book, and I've found that those who start identifying themselves as writers and authors when they first sit down to create their first draft have a higher success rate. It might sound silly, but it can give you the confidence to keep going. Having your 'why' in eye view of your writing space is also a great booster, and finding ways where you can imagine yourself holding your book in your hands is an amazing motivation booster.

Ignite & Write: The Structured Author

My mentorship client Erin Lee had a fabulous idea and mocked up a book cover with her working title on Canva, which is a free online designer software. She printed it out and stuck it on top of a hardcover book she had on her bookshelf. Because it sat next to her when she wrote, she could physically pick up 'her' book and hold it in her hands whenever she felt like her energy was dropping.

 Create a comfortable space somewhere you like spending time

Writing is easy because all you need are your notes and a laptop. You are highly portable and can set up a space anywhere you please. It could be in a home office, on a table in the dining room, patio, or a café. Without this, you will come up with all sorts of reasons why you can't sit down to write – even if it's just for half an hour.

 Embrace little rituals

I like to light scented candles when I sit down to write. So much so, that I created my own Ignite & Write line of candles! There is something about filling the room with a fragrance that just sets my creativity alight. It also works as a writer's block buster for me because whenever I feel like I've hit a rut, I can stare at the flickering flame for a moment or two. Having that distraction while I pause is enough to clear my mind of frustration and reset so I can keep going.

I also like to work with noise and if it is too quiet, I prefer to listen to music. It's interesting how each book I work on lends itself to a different soundtrack, something that I gravitate towards to help me get into the mindset of the author I am writing for or connect me to the subject matter. I didn't realise until I was interviewed by author Angela Williams and publisher Rebecca Moore on *The Gold Diggers* Podcast that seeking a noisy working environment was likely the result of my career in the newsroom, where there was a constant buzz of activity and potential for distraction.[7]

In contrast, I know writers who need absolute silence. I know writers who need to go for a run or do something physical before they sit down to write because it gets rid of excess energy so they can better focus. There are others who take a more spiritual approach and will meditate before sitting down at the computer.

Find your ritual and go with it. There is no right or wrong. Pay attention to what helps to get you in flow so you can recreate it each time you sit down to write.

 Take pause

Writing does not come naturally for every person. Even for those of us who have studied the art of words for decades, it can still be challenging to sit down, face that computer screen, and watch your words unfold – or not. This is why I encourage all emerging authors to understand the value of a simple congratulations. Make a habit of celebrating every time you give yourself the time and space to write your book. Every. Time. Even if it is only for ten minutes, congratulate yourself. By associating those happy, feel-good feelings with writing, you are making it even more attractive to sit down again and again and again. Before you know it, you can't wait for your next writing sprint to come around.

How much nicer does that feel?

Tips for writing success

I have learned a pearl of wisdom or two over many years as a professional storyteller that can help you make writing your first draft enjoyable! Like you, I am learning every day, so this is not a comprehensive collection of everything I have up my sleeve, merely a reflection of what I know at the time of writing.

I hope these tips serve you well on your writing journey and provide some answers to the questions that may threaten to slow you down by taking up valuable brain space and sapping your creative energy. If there is something bothering you that you can't find an answer to, post your question to my Facebook page and I'll answer it for you 😊

Allow yourself to feel

I'm not going to lie. Writing your story is an emotional journey. I've had tears with every one of my ghostwriting clients, but you know what? This is what builds the connection to your readers. If you recite a traumatic life experience as a factual statement,

you will completely disengage, and the power of your message is lost.

The opposite can happen, too. If what you want to write about is still too fresh or raw, you may be overcome with emotion. I can sense when writers are in this space because their words are filled with anger, resentment, blame and pain. These are all valuable emotions, but when you are still stuck *in* them, you cannot write from a place of experience or wisdom.

Yvonne Purvis, one of my superstar Ignite & Write mentees of 2023, put it perfectly when she said, 'You've got to write from the scar, not the wound.' When you are still writing from the wound, you have not yet seen the gifts the experience is giving you. As a result, your book will be excellent at capturing the events from an unfiltered perspective, but your experience is incomplete as you haven't yet come out of the other side. When you write from the scar, you have the benefit of a clear mind, an innate understanding of what you experienced and may even see why it was present in your life. You can then show what it taught you and light the way for others to learn from what you have been through.

If you feel like everything is still too raw – that you are still writing from the wound – it may be best to journal for yourself at this point. Keep writing, knowing you are documenting a real moment in time for yourself and can capture that emotion in private diaries for now.

With the passage of time, that wound will become a scar. This is when you can revisit your writing with more clarity and less clouded emotions with the aim of writing for your ideal reader and sharing the experience.

 Set goals

With only the major goal of completing your manuscript in place, it can feel like a long and unrewarding slog. Even if you are someone who isn't usually inclined to set goals or create checklists, there is great satisfaction in setting small, achievable goals. When you cross them off, there's cause to celebrate, and this can make the whole process of reaching your goal word count so much more fun!

When I am asked how long it *should* take to write your first draft, the answer is this, 'How long is a piece of string?' Not very helpful, is it? It all comes down to you. Stephen King takes three months, writing full-time. I take between three and four. But we are professional writers, and it is unusual for an aspiring author to be able to put the rest of their professional or personal commitments on hold for months on end to write their book.

Consider what your day-to-day life looks like and when you will be set aside time to write. From there, you can work out a goal timeline to have your first draft completed. Feel into this. You don't want it to be too strict in that you will be pushing yourself to the brink in order to get it done, likewise, you don't want to give yourself so much space that you can fall into procrastination because you feel like you have time to spare.

If you were to push me for a direct answer, I would say anywhere up to six months is ideal.

If you do happen to miss your timeline, don't beat yourself up over it. Carrying guilt or shame over missing days of writing or feeling like you haven't achieved what you set out to achieve in the time you set for yourself doesn't serve anybody – especially you. One of the biggest anchors for aspiring authors is this guilt. This is where being the master of your own mindset comes into play.

You can have a moment to feel guilty, but then you have to leave it in the past and move forward with fresh energy. Set a *new* goal and do your best to achieve that. Consider making the goal a little smaller – like writing 200 words a day or writing for a solid fifteen-minute block – and when you feel more confident achieving that, you can boost your word count target or the amount of time you write.

Always have multiple copies

There is no fear that compares to losing a document you have poured your heart and soul into. I vividly remember working for weeks on an essay for a university assignment and losing it to a misplaced keystroke the night before it was due. I couldn't for the life of me find the thing and had to pull an all-nighter to try to have something to submit the following afternoon.

When it comes to books, one of my mentees in 2019 lost 30,000 words she had written for her first draft. The pain was so intense from that loss that she didn't pick the project up for another two years. The thought of starting again was too much for that time, but a life-changing event sent her back to the keyboard, and she was able to complete her first draft.

Don't let this be you! Always have multiple copies of your manuscript. I now give every one of my workshop attendees a USB to save their work onto; you can also email a copy to yourself after every writing session, save it to a cloud storage platform or even work in something like Google Docs. Even though it may feel tedious to add another step to your routine, anything you can do to ensure there is a backup copy or two will be something you will never regret.

 Let consistency become your friend

Don't feel like you need to write for extended periods of time. Setting aside a day here or there can feel amazing, but chances are you won't be sitting on your rear-end writing for that entire time. When you don't, you may feel disappointed in yourself and open the door to those inner voices. Instead, set aside smaller blocks of time on a regular basis. If you miss one, it's not the end of the world. Just remember, life happens, and we have to be flexible and roll with it.

Some authors advocate for allocating a set time (where possible) so that you can train your brain to know when it's time for the creativity tap to be turned on. If your routine begins to incorporate creativity and writing as a regular feature, you will begin to start thinking about what you will write before you sit down behind the keyboard to create. This then shortens the time you need to 'get into the zone' and get in flow, which is where the magic happens.

The 'zone' is where the words flow freely from your mind, through your fingers and onto the screen without a filter. It is the process of simply channelling your thoughts and feelings and communicating them in a way that is natural to you. Believe me when I say that this is possible for anyone to achieve with dedication to maintaining a regular writing space each day.

 Quality over quantity

Let me dispel the myth that you need to sit for extended periods of time in order to be productive. This is subjective; there is no one-size-fits-all way to how much time you should allocate, so get a feel for how you work best. Some writers, like me, prefer a solid chunk of at least an hour set aside to write. This allows me to get into a flow state and to cover some ground. When time permits, I often continue writing until I find myself becoming distracted by other thoughts. That's when I know it's time to move on.

However, if writing is a new discipline for you, you may find the opposite and have to train yourself to focus on writing.

For newbies, start out with twenty-minute blocks and don't put pressure on how much you need to produce in that window of time. Sit, focus on what you want to cover for the session, and begin to write. You will find that as this becomes a daily practice, you will begin to enjoy it more, find you settle more into that magical 'flow' state, and you will want to write for longer periods of time.

If setting aside a day or weekend is more practical for you, make sure you take regular breaks to move your body and reignite that creativity and inspiration. Go for walks, have a swim, take a shower – sometimes the best inspiration lands when you aren't looking for it.

You don't have to write 'in order'

Of course, the first chapter is the most important one, but you should never feel compelled to write it first. In fact, if you are not 100 per cent clear on what your most life-changing lesson or event is for a drop-in point, I recommend that you write it towards the end of your first draft process, if not last.

It seems counterintuitive, but even if you are writing a self-contained style of book, you have to see what the rest of the journey looks like in order to capture its essence in a powerful way for the introduction. I recommend putting a pin in writing it until you have that clarity. I can guarantee that you will unearth those worthy gems as you write your first draft.

While your structure will prove invaluable for helping to focus your thoughts and place every flash of inspiration and remembered memory into its rightful place, remember that it is not immovable. If you remember a whole era of your life or learn something you think will be invaluable for your reader to know, you can absolutely adapt your structure to include it.

You may choose to add this into its own chapter or place it in an existing one to add greater depth.

Be mindful of who you let in

As a first-time author, it is common to feel like you need the approval of other people to validate what you are creating.

Writing

When you have the right people in your corner – a supportive partner, a friend, or a mentor who has a great combination of experience and empathy – you will have the perfect person to cheer you on and provide constructive criticism that will only help you to improve your writing efforts.

However, having the *wrong* person in your corner can send you into a spiral and only serve to embolden that negative self-talk that stops you from achieving your dream. Be careful who you let in on your journey. During an Ignite & Write Workshop in early 2022, one of the participants – we will call her Irene – had the most glorious idea for a book. During an era when people were battling with lockdowns, uncertainty and instability, Irene's book was going to provide a collection of uplifting spiritual stories and a way for people to feel inspired and hopeful for a greater future.

The only problem was that she had her husband as her primary support person, and he didn't believe in the same things she did. Whenever she asked him to read something, although he meant well, he would pick it to pieces from a grammatical viewpoint. This only served to diminish Irene's light and convince her that she was not good enough to be an author.

When she came to the workshop and found a supportive environment with a group of like-minded aspiring authors who *loved* the concept of her book, it was enough to lift her spirits and reengage her with the purpose that had inspired her dream in the first place. We put some boundaries in place that saw her politely remove her husband from the equation while she worked on her first draft.

Sometimes people can mean well, but it is up to you to be the gatekeeper and only let in those you feel will support and nurture your creativity.

This is especially important during the first draft stage when you can feel your most vulnerable. If you give someone a go and they aren't helping you, don't be afraid to cut them out. Surround yourself with people who uplift you and help you to connect with your purpose and authentic way of telling your story. The rest can be sorted out once the content has been created.

 Create a document called 'parking lot'

When you are writing your chapters and you come across a story, thought or quote that doesn't quite fit, put it into the parking lot. This is a great way to clear your mind so it's not holding onto these tidbits and allows you to focus wholly on your writing. When you are almost finished with your first draft, revisit the parking lot and see if some of these bits and pieces have a home within the manuscript. You may be pleasantly surprised to see there is a perfect home for some of the content that wasn't 100 per cent clear when the thought or idea first came to you!

Always be ready

You know how sometimes you get the most brilliant ideas when you are in the shower? Or in the seconds after you open your

eyes in the morning and the day-to-day thoughts haven't yet kicked into gear in your mind? What about when you go for a run or are driving to work? Inspiration tends to slap us in the face when we least expect it. As a writer, you need to be ready to bottle it when it strikes. If you have a goldfish memory like me, it is imperative that you don't waste any lightbulb moments as there is a real chance that fleeting thought will sink back down into the depths of your mind, never to resurface. Ask me how I know…

I was one of the only girls in my Scout troupe during primary school in New Zealand. I learnt a lot, one thing being the motto: 'Always be prepared'. It is a motto that has stuck in my mind all of these years. When it comes to recording your thoughts and ideas for your book, preparation is key. Being prepared to record your ideas is actually pretty simple, especially these days, thanks to the invention of smartphones. The vast majority of us carry this device around and check it incessantly throughout the day. So, why not turn it into a helpful tool for your book-writing process? Your phone will have two functions you can use – a notepad and voice memos. They will become your best friends. As soon as that inspo strikes, and you are safe to do so, whip that bad boy out and download the thought. It can be something as simple as a word, the glimmer of a concept or better still, an entire sentence that would be perfect for the opening of a chapter.

I like to think of these little insights as gifts from the universe and, if you aren't ready to accept them, they will simply be passed on to the next, more receptive, person. You miss out. Bestselling author Elizabeth Gilbert also mentioned this concept in her book *Big Magic*. Consider this: how many times have you thought you've come up with an ingenious device that will revolutionise, say, how we bake potatoes, but you do nothing? It could be years later, but sure enough, there is 'your' device being pedalled on the Shopping Channel for a princely sum. I guarantee you would be kicking yourself. It could have been you talking to that camera, your shiny white smile growing as you watch the dollars roll in.

When you are writing your own story, inspiration may come in the form of long-lost memories or connections to events in your life that may have seemed entirely separate until you started the process of becoming an author. Don't discount anything. Get it all down, as it may become a catalyst for an entire chapter or help you to strengthen the content you already have.

Remain relevant

Ideally, you want your book to be a legacy document, something people can pick up decades later and still find useful. If you are writing about a subject that has policies and regulations that are consistently being updated or modified, it's best not to go into too much detail in your book. The reason for this is that it will quickly date your book, and eventually, it will become totally irrelevant for the reader. You want your book to be evergreen!

When you are faced with this, think of other ways the reader can access the detail they need. You may choose to point them to relevant websites and send them there to access the latest information, or if this is your field of expertise, you may choose to create your own documents or website that readers can click through to. If your resources allow for it, the latter is preferable because then the readers are still on the journey with you and turning to you for the next step to get what they need.

Progress over perfectionism

When that little voice pipes to remind you that this is the first time you are taking on a project like writing a book, your inner perfectionist can rise rapidly to the surface. Please keep that perfectionist in check! I have lost count of the number of times I have heard of aspiring writers spending months on a single chapter because every time they sit down to write, they end up reading and editing what they have already written.

This messes with your flow as well as your head. Perfectionism leads to procrastination, and many people get caught up in this loop. What we are looking for is *progress*.

Perfectionism can be one of the biggest handbrakes of all. You are pumped to write, you are putting in the hours, but the progress is incredibly slow. Why? You are editing, revising and agonising over getting each sentence and paragraph perfect.

Stop!

The team of professionals you engage to help you with editing and the remainder of the publishing process will be laser-focused on these elements of your book. Your job is to be the creator; to get your life story or intellectual property onto paper.

Imagine you own three different hats. These are:

 your writing hat
 your editing hat
 your analyst hat.

While writing the SFD, you wear your writing hat. Your editing and analyst hats need to stay tucked away nicely in the cupboard while you pour every ounce of your focus into scribing your authentic story.

The analyst hat tends to creep out of the cupboard to fact-check or search for statistics right when you are in flow and making some great headway with your writing. You only want to pull this hat on when you come across a portion of writing you know will require more research or information and statistics. Save the analyst hat for a day when you aren't feeling the joy of writing.

If you allow the analyst hat to replace your writing hat when you are on a roll, you will find yourself in a Google rabbit hole as you click through from one article to another. Before you know it, you've spent an hour or more not actually achieving anything when you were writing effortlessly earlier in that day's session.

When I feel the analyst hat beginning to flutter, I make a note in my document. I either add a comment, which appears on the side of the document, away from the main working space, or I highlight the section and simply carry on with writing. When you have a day where writing is the last thing on Earth you feel like doing (believe me, they come), you can pull out your analyst hat

and start to tackle those niggling tasks. They require a different side of the brain to your creative component, and you will still be making progress on your manuscript. It's a win-win!

What I'd love for you to be striving for is progress over perfectionism. Taking any type of step forward every day will help you to reach your goal quicker than you think.

As a writer, I know it's not always as simple as sitting down and telling your brain, 'Okay, it's time to write'. There will be days when you simply cannot string a coherent sentence together. Don't beat yourself up about this; it can happen to the best in the business.

Writer's block is valid and can be a real handbrake on your creative process, so make sure you check out the chapter dedicated to busting through these blocks later in the book.

Now that you know there are multiple hats you *could* be wearing, leave the editing and analyst hat in the closet. In fact, your editing hat should only see the light of day once you have finished your SFD and the time has come to read through your entire manuscript.

> Done is better than perfect when it comes to your first draft.

Perfectionism is a writer's greatest enemy. Too many writers never get started because they worry the end result won't live up to their expectations.

Don't let this stop you from writing. Because here's the thing: no matter how much time you spend on your first draft, it's going to need some work.

In the beginning, focus on *what* you want to say rather than *how* you want to say it. Just get all your thoughts down on the page, and then once your first draft is written, you can go back and make the necessary changes.

Finding your voice

When fear is peering over your shoulder, whispering that you're not good enough, professional enough or qualified enough, you may be tempted to try to become someone else between the covers of your book. You want to become someone you *think* people will like better.

You might want to sound like an academic when the idea of research and being serious makes you squirm a little. Likewise, you may want to write with humour when your jokes often fall flat in real life.

When we try to reshape who we are in the pages of our books, we step – often subconsciously – down the path of inauthenticity. These small steps, which take us further from our true selves, can mount up over time and lead readers to disengage. Readers can sense that disconnect.

People have well-honed bullshit radars these days, it's a sign of the times we are living in, and if there is any whiff of inauthenticity, they will move on to someone who is more congruent.

Writing

Please realise the brilliance of who you are and what you have to share with the world!

The fact of the matter is we are all unique, and we all have our own way of communicating and expressing ourselves in the world.

Readers will pick up your book to learn about you in the way you would communicate with your friends. I am a huge consumer of autobiographies. Yes, I read these books for professional development (I want to see what bestsellers are made of!), but autobiographies also satisfy my incessant curiosity about humans and what drives each one of us. What I find time and again is the most successful books are those that are written with the author's authentic voice.

Mark Brandon 'Chopper' Read was an Australian convicted criminal, gang member and author who wrote a series of semi-autobiographical fictional crime novels, as well as children's books. He was renowned for his crude and unfiltered language, so imagine, for a moment, that he released books with eloquent prose and poetic flow. He would be laughed out of town, and rightly so. Chopper built a following on his incredibly rough around the edges persona and to present himself as anything other than that would go as far against the grain you possibly could.

Yes, you will need a professional editor to polish your writing and ensure it is grammatically sound before you release your book to your eager readers, but balancing editing with authenticity is vital. Your editor should be able to identify your tone of voice and personality and ensure they remain intact. After all, capturing the essence of your authentic self is the most important thing you can do to make your book unique.

Let's look at some examples. Topic-wise, I'll go with perceptions of women, which fits with two autobiographies I have read: Tina Fey's *Bossypants* and Glennon Doyle's *Untamed*. These women have two different ways of expressing themselves.

Glennon is spiritual, and to pull just one passage from her wisdom, she writes:

> 'The beauty industry convinces us that our thighs, frizz, skin, fingernails, lips, eyelashes, leg hair, and wrinkles are repulsive and must be covered and manipulated, so we learn to not trust the bodies we live in.'[8]

In comparison, Tina, who is a comedian, actress and renowned director, writes this:

> 'I think the first real change in women's body image came when JLo turned it butt-style. That was the first time that having a large-scale situation in the back was part of mainstream... and then what felt like moments later, boom – Beyonce brought the leg meat. A back porch and thick muscular legs were now widely admired.'[9]

You would be jolted beyond belief if you opened the pages of Glennon's book and found a quote like Tina's, and vice versa. Staying authentic in the way you deliver your story is the key to connecting with the readers, who want to learn, be inspired and go on the journey with *you*.

Drawing out your authentic voice

Similar to the exercise you went through to assure yourself of your authentic voice in Book One, *The Mindful Author*, I also give future authors this exercise in my mentorship program:

1. Think about one of the most emotional events you have experienced in your life. Now, emotional doesn't automatically have to be sad. It could be a moment when you almost wet your pants or snorted milk out of your nose because it was so hilarious. It could be a moment when you were so filled with joy or love that you thought you could have sworn you were levitating off the ground. It could be a moment when you were so angry that your blood was boiling, and you would have given the Incredible Hulk a run for his money in the boxing ring.

2. *Feel* it. Slide back into your skin at that moment in time.

3. Now write. Don't make your sentence structure perfect. Just write from that emotion as if you were explaining it to one of your closest friends or family members.

4. Let it pour out for as long as you need to. Don't stop to read it. Stopping will cut off your flow and move you from your emotions and into your head – the killer of creativity.

5. When you are finished, walk away from your notepad or computer.

6. Get a coffee, make a snack, go for a walk or just be still for a moment. When you come back, you are allowed to read through what you have just written.

7. Be amazed. This is your truest form of expression, and you have done it without having to do anything more than trust your emotions and communicate through them.

Whenever you feel yourself questioning whether your writing or voice is good enough, just remember that there is someone out there just waiting to hear your message exactly the way you are going to tell it.

Show, don't tell

In a nutshell, the difference is that 'show' invokes a mental image of a scene or emotion, while 'tell' is a direct statement of an action and/or emotion.

Basically, instead of telling the reader every little detail, you can engage some techniques that paint a picture, allowing the

reader to fill in the gaps. This can be extremely powerful and works to draw the reader in and connect them at a deeper level to your story.

You will notice the vast majority of fiction books rely on the show don't tell concept, but it is also a great tool to use when you write your nonfiction book. It reminds you that your readers are intelligent people, and you don't have to give them every single descriptor – or 'tell' – them everything in black and white. It's about painting the picture and then encouraging the theatre of the mind to take over.

Remember when you read a book that engaged you so intensely that you were able to create that world in your head? That is theatre of the mind at its best.

While telling is all part of the writing process, the trick is not to fall into consistently explaining everything, taking away the reader's opportunity to fill in the blanks. If your inner voice is piping up with 'but I'm not a good writer...' right now, let me reassure you that you do not have to mess with your authentic voice in any way to achieve this. All it takes is some little tweaks, which can be made once you finish your first draft.

For example, if you or someone in your story is angry, writing, 'Bob was angry' is telling.

To show, you would paint more of a picture, 'Bob stormed into the room, his face flushed red, and slammed his fist on the table'.

See the difference?

Your readers will *know* Bob is angry; they have been able to deduce that by being shown. This can be used for just about any form of emotion or state of being. If Bob is tall, he may have to duck to get through a doorway. If he is tired, he could have puffy eyes and be unable to stop yawning.

These small language tweaks are often enough to steer you out of telling territory and give your reader a chance to engage their imagination.

There is a line in Australian tennis champion Jelena Dokic's memoir, *Unbreakable* that really sucker-punched me in the gut. 'The belt is brown, its leather thick and hard, it feels as sharp as a knife when it's whipped against my skin.' It comes on page thirty-four, so the reader already knows her father has a temper that transforms into physical rage when he is displeased. Instead of telling her readers that her father was preparing to beat her again, Jelena and ghostwriter Jessica Halloran chose to 'show' how ominous it was when the belt made an appearance.

The second powerful way to 'show' your reader is to use the five senses. How do things:

-  taste?
- feel?
- smell?
- look?
- sound?

Not all five senses will be relevant for every situation, so zoom in on the most relevant ones for that moment.

Writing

For example, Bob may have just come back from a very long run, but instead of saying that outright, you might write.

'Bob struggled to catch his breath as he shuffled through the door, his flushed cheeks almost glowing.'

Writing about action and reaction is also a great way to show your reader what is happening. Instead of describing the personality traits of someone in your book, show your reader through how they act and react to what happens around them. This will reveal their unique characteristics without you explicitly having to tell your reader.

Instead of writing, 'Bob was a bad man', you could write, 'Bob strode around with a permanent scowl on his face; he wouldn't hesitate to kick a cat if it got too close'.

Make the most of body language and facial expressions, too. We are always very physical in the way that we talk and interact with others, so see how you can incorporate this into your writing.

The third powerful strategy to deploy is the spoken word. Conversation permeates our lives every day. Verbal communication allows us to connect with the people around us, develop relationships and build trust. It is also the main vehicle through which we can channel our emotions – the good and the bad.

Conversations can make or break happiness. They can build up or break down. We take on many of the things that have been said to us throughout our lifetimes. Often, these things become the basis of who we tell ourselves we are. They are the foundations of the stories we tell ourselves – for better or for worse.

All of these reasons are why including dialogue in your manuscript is one of the most powerful ways to build connection with your reader.

You can capture so much more in a conversation between two people than you could describing what is unfolding.

In just a couple of lines, you can deduce how people are feeling, what their personality is like and what the power dynamics of the people look like. You can get a glimpse into their psyche and perhaps even relate to the words and how they are delivered.

What's more, conversations unfold in real-time, so the immediacy of the interaction can also serve to pick up the pace of your story.

You don't have to fill an entire page with dialogue to pack a big punch. Sometimes, single lines, when delivered in the right context, can speak volumes. Take a scene where a person has just found out they have an incurable illness:

'I'm sorry, there's nothing more we can do', the doctor whispered, unable to meet my gaze.

Remember, when you 'show' your readers something, you are making them work for the story. They will need to put some

effort into building that picture in their mind, feeling that emotion and jumping into the pages alongside you.

It is equally important not to fall into the trap of thinking that every single sentence has to be embellished as if you are creating an over-the-top movie script. 'Showing' is to be deployed when you want to elevate those more powerful moments in your story to the next level.

So how do you know where those moments are?

When to show and when to tell

Here are some guidelines you can use to determine if it's beneficial to spend a little more energy 'showing' your reader something rather than 'telling' them.

Show if:

- it is a pivotal moment in your story.
- you want to bring the reader into the scene and know it will be more powerful to describe more of the details of the setting or the characters so they can picture it.
- there is a conflict, drama or crisis unfolding, equally, it could be a moment of pure joy, elation and connection.
- you are presenting an important conversation and, dialogue would be more powerful than describing an interaction.

Tell if:

- you are providing information that the reader needs to know but isn't critical to developing your story.
- you are linking two events together, you don't need to go as in-depth with the details.
- you need to provide context to a situation.

It will take some effort to incorporate the 'show' elements into your writing, so don't worry if it doesn't come naturally while writing your first draft. If you're worried that you're telling too much and not showing enough, but your writing still flows well and engages readers, don't feel obligated to change it!

When you are finished with your shitty first draft, have a little break and then take a look through your work in its entirety. Yes! This is when you can allow your editor hat to come out to play. More importantly, you will be able to identify the sections of your manuscript that could use more 'oompf' to boost the power of particular scenes. You can also look at your paragraphs with a more refined approach to see where you can transform telling words into descriptive and emotive words that reel the reader in.

Repurposing content

Diaries, programs, articles, blogs, podcasts, interviews. What do all of these things have in common? They are all forms of content you can repurpose in your book.

When you have poured your heart and soul into creating content either for yourself or for the public, it can become a goldmine when the time comes to write a book.

Take a look at all of the content you have already created, and you may realise that you have been 'writing your book' long before you realised you were!

A beautiful soul who completed the online Ignite & Write Workshop had kept the diaries she had written while she was undergoing treatment for both of her breast cancer diagnoses, a journey that spanned around seven years. When the time came to write her book, these diaries provided her direct access back to the highly emotional state she was in at the time. This allowed her to capture the authentic essence of who she was; without the veil of the healed mind we often have to look back on experiences with. At the time, she was writing from the wound, but when she completed the online workshop, enough time had passed that she was ready to write from the scar.

Joanne Wilson, who wrote *Renovate Your Relationship*, was able to create strong foundations for her book using columns she had written for a newspaper.[10] She was also the host of a regular radio segment and used topics inspired by listeners, who would send her emails to ask their personal questions, to drive the content for her show. Knowing the challenges and common questions people had, Jo knew the content within her columns and radio segments would be perfect for a book.

To transform them into a written-word format (which is so important because the spoken word can use intonation, emphasis and other verbal cues that are difficult to replicate in the written word), Jo crafted chapters and added new insights and research. In fact, it was the suggestion from someone else that she use her columns to create a book that planted the seed for her to become a published author in the first place!

As we covered in the Collaboration section earlier, five-time author Zoe Sparks also had a 'lightbulb moment' when she saw how she could collate the stories shared by 52 women over the course of a year through her business community newsletter and create an inspiring book for businesswomen.

If you have been posting regular blogs to a website, on social media, or interviewing people who have amazing insights into your relevant industry or subject, keep in mind that it is all content you can use in your book. Never underestimate the power of these resources or worry about releasing the same content. It will be completely new to some, and for those who may have read or heard the content before, when it is placed in the context of the rest of your book, it will only become more poignant and powerful.

You may even have been delivering a workshop or well-developed keynote speech that has been inspiring people. This was the case for Catherine Molloy, the author of *The Million Dollar Handshake*, who was a guest on my *Ignite & Write* podcast.

Writing

'I'm a big strategy person and started delivering workshops on body language, mindset, behaviours and had the million-dollar handshake keynote I'd been delivering for a few years about the way we connect and communicate, even in those first seven seconds. You know our first impression does really matter! Anyway, I was... about to meet Hachette, which is a book company that had heard about my talk and thought it would be really great having a woman create this book on *The Million Dollar Handshake*. I had the meeting and got the first chapter off to the publisher, and the rest is really history.'

You can listen to her full interview here:

Creation vs generation

While writing this book, I was asked in two different environments what my thoughts are on the use of artificial intelligence (AI) as a book-writing tool. I was first asked by one of the members of the three-strong judging panel of the 2023 Sunshine Coast Business Awards, followed by one of the aspiring authors in my last Ignite & Write Workshop for that year.

There's no doubt that AI is here to stay. The number of webinars, workshops and programs popping up in my social media newsfeeds teaching people how to use AI is growing every week. The temptation is there for people who might want to take the gondola to the author summit rather than walking it themselves.

I have seen webinars that encourage people to generate 'books' using AI and list them on Amazon as a form of money-making scheme. But guess what? These types of books will rarely lead to clients for other elements of your business or repeat readers (if you choose to publish subsequent books). Why? Because they lack any form of connection.

> I don't feel threatened by AI, and I don't believe any creative writer should be.

Sure, AI can be an important tool for businesses but when it comes to books; there is a real difference between something that is *generated* by AI and something that is *created* by someone like you.

AI tools can generate copy in the blink of an eye, but it is drawn from a bank of knowledge, and anything produced will be generic. From speaking with those who have used it for historical research, it is clear that AI draws from websites like Wikipedia, which relies on users to add content, which often means it isn't even a factual source.

Most importantly, AI content lacks soul and will never be able to replicate your authentic voice or provide something unique for you. It is not a creative process at all; it's the equivalent of

outsourcing to a poor contractor who will google your subject matter and pull something together from that.

However, when you *create*, you will always outshine anything that is generated by AI. You will write with your unique voice, know how to communicate directly to your ideal reader and draw on personal experience and knowledge you may have learned from the school of hard knocks rather than a textbook. This is what makes books shine.

I would bet that just about anyone would be able to pick up a book created by an author and another generated by AI and be able to spot the difference almost immediately. The former comes from the heart and soul, something AI has yet to – and may never – master.

What you are doing is creating. What you are making is unique. There will never be another book out there that is exactly like yours. Your book is the kind that will create an impact, stay in the hearts of your readers and start a ripple effect of positive change. Don't ever think that AI can do a better job than you can!

Hiding real people in real stories

Sadly, there are many potential books languishing half-written, or worse, not even given the oxygen needed to breathe life into words on the page. Why? Because the author is stuck in fear – *what will X think?*

X is anyone, everyone, a particular person.

Ignite & Write: The Structured Author

The fact is, as much as your story is about you, there are always going to be supporting 'characters' who feature in your story. Some of them may have been mentors or heroes in their own right. Others, not so much.

It is usually the latter that causes fear to gnaw away at your writing process. You want to share your unbridled truth, but you hold back because of uncertainty. This is such a huge barrier for so many aspiring authors, which is why I presented a library series in 2024 addressing this topic.

A book will rarely only feature one person with a singular voice throughout. Therefore, it is necessary to include other people or characters who are integral to telling your authentic story.

While fiction writers have carte blanche to create characters with specific physical characteristics and personality traits to fit their style of story, the good news is that nonfiction characters will already be fully formed as they are real-life people.

All you then have to do is tap into the unique personality traits of each of your characters and highlight the role they play in your story. Who are the pivotal characters? Which characters pop in for a short season, or even a moment, to provide support or guidance on your quest?

The longer the character remains in your book, the more the reader will be able to connect with them on an emotional level, just as they will to you, the main protagonist of your own story.

As I shared in Book One, there are going to be instances where you decide changing the names or obscuring the identities of

Writing

some of the people featured in your book might be the best way forward. It may help you to protect someone's privacy or identity, or maybe even to protect your own safety. It may also be because you have asked for permission to write about them, but they have declined.

> It is important to note that obscuring someone's identity or changing their name does not give you free rein to write whatever you want about them.

Consider the three knee-jerk reactions aspiring authors can have when they fear upsetting someone in their book:

1. 'I'll just write a novel instead.'
2. 'I'll write under a pseudonym.'
3. 'I'll just chop out the part that includes them.'

They all sound like easy solutions, but will they serve the purpose of your book?

As with any choice, there are pros and cons, so I would like to bring awareness to them for you:

 'I'll just write a novel instead.'

Pros: In nonfiction, it is key to remain as factual as possible. Pushing the boundaries too much will push you into 'faction,' which is a fictional book based on fact. I have seen authors such as Alex Gerrick with *A Season of Thunder* successfully use this method to tell stories that showcase the lives of ancestors as they cannot know true dialogue or much beyond the bare minimum historical facts.

I have also worked with aspiring authors who want to share their lived experience with a level of disconnect and choose to venture into fiction territory, a la Trent Dalton's bestselling *Boy Swallows Universe*. This can be a wonderful way to create something unique and entertaining and you can't argue with Dalton's success! It serves as an easy way to share their story without 'outing' the people in their lives.

Cons: One of my favourite Dalton anecdotes is that people always look at his hands at live events. In *Boy Swallows Universe*, the character based on Dalton loses a finger when it is severed in a drug lord retribution act. Dalton has all of his fingers in real life. If you envision using your book as a pillar for business or a way to open doors to paid opportunities to educate or inspire, venturing into fiction muddies the potency of your message as the reader will never truly know what was real and what was improvised.

 'I'll write under a pseudonym.'

Pros: By writing under a pen name, you are adding an extra layer of disconnection between yourself as the author and the people you write about in your book.

Cons: You can get tripped up big time when you reach the marketing phase. This is a vital part of your authorship journey

and requires you to step out from behind your keyboard and become the 'face' of your book. Try as you might, you will not be able to go on television, or have a photographer come out to take your photo for a newspaper or magazine article because you will not be able to show your face.

If your purpose is to make an impact, you want to get your book into the hands of as many people as possible and I have seen many an author hamstring themselves because they chose to hide behind a pseudonym.

 'I'll just chop out the part that includes them.'

Pros: If you don't write it, no one can read it. Problem solved!

Cons: If the people or the situations are vital to provide context for your reader, you are doing a huge disservice to remove them. I had this happen with a client who I'll call Eva. She had written her first draft and when I read it through for a structural edit, there were several places where I noticed gaps in time and statements that alluded to something without being bold enough to state it, as if she was glossing over the surface. I highlighted all of these and when I went through the manuscript with her.

She blushed and admitted straight away that she had been deliberate in leaving anything out that related to her parents. She didn't want to write about them as she knew they would be upset.

The issue with this was, the *context* was vital. Eva's story was about leaving home as a teenager to live on the streets. I wouldn't imagine anyone would leave a calm, safe home environment to sleep rough. Bringing in her home life was vital for the reader to understand why she made the choices that she did. Without that context, they could never truly connect with Eva. We were able to work together to define which situations involving her parents were relevant to share.

Through this, we could *show* the reader her home environment and they would have a clear understanding of Eva's decision without her having to label her parents in any way.

If you are still unsure where you stand on whether or not to hide someone here's a hint: come back to your 'why'.

To hide or not to hide?

My first book provides tips on how to approach people and seek approval to include them in your book. With permission – *always* in writing – you have covered your bases. We often assume how someone will react to being written about by someone else. You may be met with excitement. You may be met with agreement and a few conditions, such as changing their name or allowing them to read it before publishing. You may be met with anger or an outright no. The truth is, you never know until you ask.

Once you have the answer, you can decide on the best course of action – continue on anyway, or find ways to hide them in your book.

I have worked with people who have escaped abusive relationships or need to write about people that they cannot, or simply do not want to, seek permission from.

Writing

The good news is, you can absolutely write your truth in a way that negates ever having to get that permission, but there are some rules that should not be broken:

- Avoid the blame game at all costs. Finger-pointing, justification and blame will not serve you in any way, shape or form. It is petty, and your readers will disconnect if they sense that you are not prepared to own your own actions. We all have those moments in our lives when we could have chosen a better path.
- Don't attempt to put the reader into the mind of another person. You can never truly *know* what they were thinking or feeling. You can only give your best *guess*, and that is where your book shifts into the danger zone.
- Write how *you* perceived the events to have unfolded, describing how it made you feel and the lessons you took away from it. Just as you can't articulate what someone else is thinking or feeling, they can't do the same to you.
- Stick to facts. You cannot write, 'Jason was so dodgy. I know he was stealing money from the till because my brother-in-law's cousin saw him pull out wads of fifties at the pub.' This is based on hearsay. You can, however, include the fact that money went missing. 'I was panicking because every Friday night, the till was out by a couple of hundred dollars.'
- If an event has been documented in the media or in court and there is a public record of it, you can absolutely use these facts in your book. Do this

without embellishing and twisting things to make them more dramatic.

 Don't be tempted to play with the truth so either you or others can save face. If you are presenting a nonfiction book, remain true to the facts.

 It probably goes without saying, but publishing any confidential or classified information will only get you into trouble.

 If you have signed a non-disclosure agreement, it is my strong recommendation that you honour it.

Defamation

Coming from a print media background, I had the legal requirements of reporting drummed into me pretty darn quick. Once something is in print, it is there forever. Books are no different.

Upsetting people is not a legal issue, but defamation is. Defamation is one of the most common legal issues authors can encounter – the second is breach of copyright, which you can avoid by thoroughly referencing any quotes and researched information you may use. The definition of defamation is 'the act of damaging the good reputation of someone'.[11] Now this sounds pretty vague, but when you look at what an aggrieved person needs to prove in order to take legal action, it becomes clearer.

A defamation claim can be made by someone if:

 the material is not supported by facts

the person or business was clearly identified

 the material caused, or is continuing to cause, 'serious harm' to their reputation.

To use extreme examples, you wouldn't call someone a paedophile or a murderer in your book unless they had been tried and convicted of such offences.

The defamation case of Amber Heard versus Johnny Depp that played out on the international stage in 2022 stemmed from an opinion piece Heard wrote for *The Washington Post* in 2018. Interestingly, in that same article, Heard wrote:

> 'The president of our country has been accused by more than a dozen women of sexual misconduct, including assault and harassment.'

But she wasn't taken to court by Donald Trump, who was the US president at the time. Why? Because the accusations had been widely reported and are on the public record.

Instead, Heard was taken to court by her ex-husband Depp because she referred to herself as a 'public figure representing domestic abuse' and how she had seen 'in real time' how society protected people in power who were abusive.

Although she did not mention Depp by name, Heard wrote that she became a domestic violence figure two years earlier. Because she was still married to Depp at this time, this alluded to him being the alleged abuser. At the time, it was not supported by facts on the public record and Depp claimed it harmed his reputation and career as he was losing sponsorship and movie contracts. The defamation case made international headlines as so much of their private lives was made public. This is because the court had to determine whether there was sufficient fact to support her claims of domestic abuse.

> This is a reminder of the power of language when you are writing about other people.

As a little side note, you cannot defame someone who is deceased, and no, their descendants cannot sue you for defamation either. This frees up a lot of people who are writing their family histories!

The way defamation laws are structured varies in each country and even in states within countries, so I recommend you seek advice from a lawyer if you have major concerns.

It is always better to err on the side of caution, and while it may be an undesirable expense upfront, it can pay off if a consultation with a lawyer saves you from addressing concerns notices (the initial stages of a defamation suit) or litigation.

When you absolutely cannot identify someone

While defamation is actioned by a third party who may appear in your book if you do not take the proper precautions, there are instances where you absolutely *cannot* identify someone – even if you wanted to.

Writing

Governments and court judges can install gag orders (also known as suppression orders) at their discretion. What this does is restrict names, information or comments from being made public in any way. It is primarily used to protect ongoing operations and investigations or to protect the privacy of victims or minors. When the identity of the perpetrator reveals who the victim or minors are, they can also be covered under the order.

A judge may also issue a gag order to prevent attorneys or witnesses from talking about the case to the public in order to prevent pre-trial prejudice. In this instance, the order may be lifted once the trial has been completed. Others can remain in place for up to 30 years.

Please note that I am not a legal expert. The information provided is for general informational purposes only. If you need legal advice, please consult a qualified attorney.

If you are unsure if there are any legal restrictions placed around judicial proceedings you wish to write about, you can:

- Search online for information about the trial and see if there is any mention of a suppression order. You can use resources like Google Scholar and every country will have its own national database of court proceedings that you can access.
- Search for any news articles released by traditional media outlets. If they have withheld identifying information or have mentioned closed court, you will know there are orders in place.

Contact the court where the trial took place and ask if there were any gag orders in place and if so, how long they are in force for.

 If you were involved in the trial or have a legal interest in the case, consult a lawyer. They can also provide you with advice on how to proceed.

If you have been part of a judicial process and signed non-disclosure agreements, you also are bound to that contract and will not be able to write about anything that is linked to that agreement. Doing so will be a breach of that contract – you could be liable.

As mentioned earlier, you also cannot identify someone as being any type of criminal if they have not been convicted of those crimes.

Pseudonyms

As previously discussed, there are risks associated with using pseudonyms or not clearly identifying each character. That said, if you can't work around it, there are a few tips and tricks to ensure strong character development – and accuracy.

There have been many times when I've had an aspiring author who ended up giving one person two new names or even giving the same pseudonym to two different people! This not only risks confusing the reader and your story, but it presents a nightmare for your editor to have to untangle exactly who is who.

I highly recommend writing your first draft with everyone's real names. When you've completed your first draft, create a table that clearly shows the person's real name and their new name.

To save time, you can download a Pseudonym Template from the Ignite & Write Resource Centre here:

If you are struggling to come up with your own names, you can take a look at your bookshelf and borrow the first or last names from your favourite authors (not both in the same combination!) or your favourite shows or movies. I've asked my kids for names at times because they are never short of ideas!

You can choose whether or not you share this list with your editor, or you take on the responsibility of changing everything before the editor first sees your manuscript. Keep this document in multiple safe places (one on your computer, one printed out in your office and one on a USB or cloud platform) so that you will always be able to keep track of who's who once you have made the changes.

There are a few key rules to follow when choosing pseudonyms:

   Don't pick a new name that starts with the same letters. This applies to for both their first and last name.

   Avoid anything that rhymes with their real name.

   Stay away from pet names or nicknames you may have used for them or they have been known by within the family or wider community.

I have seen great success with authors who have been able to create powerful connections to both heroes and villains in their supporting 'characters', even by calling them something whimsical like Mr Kentucky or Ms Polka Dots.

There are many other strategies you can tap into, such as Paris Hilton's use of physical characteristics to 'name' the wardens she writes about in *Paris: The memoir*. She was able to name the institutions she was sent away to as a young woman and openly describe the abuse she faced there as they had already been openly investigated and publicised. What she couldn't name, however, were the individuals who worked in those institutions.

Hilton cleverly chose descriptors that painted a vivid picture in your mind (not always flattering) knowing that it would be highly improbable that any of the guards would 'out' themselves by voicing their objection to her chosen name for them.

Writing

Omission can sometimes be just as effective. In the case of Prince Harry's memoir *Spare*, he chose not to name the woman he lost his virginity to as a teenager. He still told the story and even though it was only a few paragraphs out of a few hundred pages, it definitely had an impact! The whole world was trying to guess who this woman was and, in the end, she chose to 'out' herself to the world's media.

If you definitely need to hide someone, have a play around with different approaches to see what feels good for your style of book. Because this is so subjective, we spend a fair bit of time on this during the Ignite & Write Mentorship to find the right fit for each writer's story.

'I think perfectionism is just fear in fancy shoes and a mink coat, pretending to be elegant when actually it's just terrified. Because underneath that shiny veneer, perfectionism is nothing more than a deep existential angst that says, again and again, 'I am not good enough and I will never be good enough'.'

Elizabeth Gilbert, from her book *Big Magic*

Beating writer's block

Ignite & Write: The Structured Author

You stare at an unforgiving cursor as it blinks on your screen atop a completely blank page. It taunts you. Makes you feel like you are not good enough to call yourself an author. How can you when you can't even string a single sentence together?

In another situation, you have been on a roll. The words have been pouring out of you, and you feel like you have finally gotten the hang of this writing thing. You sit down excitedly for your next writing session and start to pick up the pace, and then… nothing. Your mind goes completely blank. It's as if some alien has entered your brain and sucked every coherent thought out of your mind, and there it is, that freakin' blinking cursor again.

Don't despair! Writer's block hits even the most seasoned writers, so you can expect it to rear its ugly head at some stage during your writing journey.

I know from a creative point of view, there are days when I can smash out thousands of words and others when I am distracted by absolutely anything and go into my goldfish memory mode. If you have those days, don't force the writing. When you reach the point of forcing it, you suck out all the fun, and then the idea of completing a manuscript becomes a chore. Instead, embrace the days when you are in flow and fully commit to them.

On days when you feel like writing is akin to poking yourself in the eye with a hot iron rod, look at what else you can do to progress your book. You may be able to:

- Search for quotes that might fit perfectly with chapters in your book.
- Collate photos or graphics you might like to use in your book and pop them into their own folder.

Beating writer's block

- Make a list of people you need to reach out to for approval to mention in your book and start to email them to get written permission.
- Go back through your manuscript to date and look for areas where you have left yourself notes to fill in missing pieces or add statistics.
- Get your research on and learn more about your subject – you may hit on some new insights you can touch on in your book.
- Have fun with potential cover images or designs.
- Engage with your future readers by posting to social media or emailing them with an update on your book project or a teaser of what's to come.

Any one of these little tasks will keep your mind on your book and help you to progress at the same time.

No matter whether you are a first-time writer or you do it professionally, writer's block is a part of the creative process. While we know this with our logical minds, it doesn't stop our subconscious from kicking in with comments like:

'You're never going to be good at writing. Who do you think you are? Writing a book! Ha! No one's going to read that! You can't even complete a single chapter, so you may as well give up now.'

Every writer has had those thoughts at some stage of their creative process. So, what's the key to overcoming this fear of the blank page? To understand that what you write doesn't have to be perfect.

Getting caught up in perfection is *the* number one thing that stops people from writing their books. The worry that every sentence has to sound like it flowed from the pen of Brene Brown or has the motivation-boosting power of Tony Robbins can stifle any original creativity that is waiting to burst forth from your fingers.

Guess what? It only has to sound like you.

You have an authentic and natural way of storytelling, and when you come back to that very basic concept, you will be able to tell your stories and share your message in a way that only you can.

This is what the world needs – you! Not some version of you that you think everyone else wants.

So, I challenge you to share more of your authentic self when you next sit down to write. You've got this!

Check your state of mind

When you boil it down to the very core, writer's block is simply a state of mind. If you sit down and have already decided you don't know what you are going to tackle for the writing session, you are already blocking your natural ability to tap into your creativity.

Don't self-sabotage. Instead, ask yourself:

- 'What amazing story am I going to uncover today?'
- 'Where am I being called to write today?'
- 'What would really light me up if I told that particular story today?'

Beating writer's block

Find ways to clear your mind of distractions so you can provide an unobstructed pathway for the memories, thoughts and feelings that are associated with your story to come through. This could be accomplished through a short meditation, simple mindfulness practices, even getting some exercise in before you sit down to write.

Watch how the writer's block melts away when you reconnect with your passion and purpose.

Clear out the clutter

You've sat down to write content for your book but once again found there's just too much rolling around in your mind to focus on a single train of thought. You are a busy person, juggling many roles and responsibilities. Sometimes, the to-do list resides in your mind, putting a handbrake on your ability to access your creativity to write your book.

It can be as frustrating as anything and may be sending you into a spiralling writer's block. Rest assured, it's more common than you think, and even better, there is a simple solution to clear your mind: the humble brain dump.

I am a huge advocate for structure when writing your book, so the brain dump is not how you would approach writing your whole manuscript, but it is an invaluable tool to clear out the clutter in your mind and can be deployed whenever you need it.

How does it work?

Five simple steps to clear your brain

Step 1: Get a pen or pencil and paper (Yup! We are going old school).

Step 2: Set a timer for 90 seconds.

Step 3: Write down every thought that is bugging you. Whatever pops into your head, write it down. It doesn't have to be related to your book – hang out the washing, respond to grandma's letter, sign up for Ignite & Write Workshop. 😉 These are all acceptable things to get out of your mind.

Step 4: Once the time is up, marvel at your list. See if there is anything on there that is relevant for your book that you can now expand on with your writing session.

If not, celebrate your clear mind and turn your attention to writing, knowing that you won't forget anything on your to-do list because it is all written down for you.

Step 5: If you still feel that mind chatter going on, set the time for another 90 seconds and go again!

Change your environment

Sometimes, no matter how hard you try, the words just don't come to you. So, instead of staring at a blank screen, try some of these techniques:

- Stand up and stretch your legs.
- Go have a cup of tea or coffee.
- Do the dishes.
- Take a walk outside.
- Change your mental environment and find something else to do that will progress your book project without writing.

You might be thinking, *what? She's telling me to walk away from my computer?!*

Yes, if you have no other actions to take, highlighted facts to check or content to research, sometimes a change of scenery, even if it's just for a few minutes, is all it takes to spark some new ideas.

When you sit back down to your computer, you'll be in a better frame of mind, and the words should come a little easier. If the time comes, give it a try!

Utilise your structure

One of the more challenging parts of writing your first draft is coming up with a good opening.

Guess what? There are no rules about the order you need to write your book in. The reader will likely read it from start to finish, but you don't have to create it that way!

Because this is a creative endeavour, everyone's processes will vary. Some are hamstrung unless they write from beginning to end. It may sound counterintuitive, but I always write the first chapter last. This is because I shape the flow of the manuscript as I work through the other chapters. By the time I'm finished, I know what the logical entry point is for the reader. If there is a powerful hook somewhere in the middle of the book, I will bring it forward and create a cyclic structure. This middle now becomes the intro, and readers will be met with something profound and powerful to hook them in.

If there's nothing that jumps out at you as the definite opening chapter, write chronologically until your perfect introduction reveals itself to you with a metaphorical slap in the face. I love nothing more than the 'a-ha' moment that comes with a healthy dose of goosebumps as confirmation you've found the right moment.

Time management

We've all told ourselves we'll write later or that we'll do 'just one more thing' and then get started. Before you know it, four days have passed, and you haven't written a single word. (No joke, I've helped an author to release the memoir she had procrastinated on writing for four *decades*.)

When you're experiencing a bout of writer's block, it's easy to procrastinate. Treat writing as part of your daily routine, like showering and brushing your teeth. Scheduling time will force you (in the best possible way) to keep that time sacred and keep procrastination at the door. You are the only person who can keep distractions at bay during your scheduled writing times and also ensure that even when life happens, you don't just keep pushing your writing times back further and further.

Beating writer's block

We all have the same twenty-four hours in a day, but what sets successful authors apart from those who simply dream about becoming an author is their investment in time.

 ### Set a schedule

Try to write at the same time every day. This does not have to be a single sitting! If you are juggling it with a day job and other activities, you can have smaller writing sprints in the morning, at night, or any time.

 ### Use a timer

Don't feel like you have to sit for hours on end to have a productive writing session. You can achieve just as much (for some people, more!) in shorter, concentrated bursts. If you feel like longer sessions haven't been working for you, set a timer for 20 minutes. Don't do anything but write. Take a five-minute break, then give yourself another 20 minutes. If this works for you, keep going with it!

 ### Set a goal for each session

Instead of looking at an overall word count goal, how about dialling it back and setting a goal for each session you sit down for? Having micro goals will allow you many more small wins when you can tick it off as done.

 ### Avoid multitasking

Turn off the phone, stop your email from pinging and make sure your workspace is distraction-free. The world won't end during your writing session;

everything else can be dealt with once you have completed your writing goal for the day.

 Create an opportunity for wins

Even if you aren't normally a list person, give to-do lists a try to keep you on track and remove the stress of trying to remember everything that needs to be done for your next chapter. This also creates another opportunity for wins.

Procrastination

Procrastination is one of the toughest things to overcome. It's true that we will find all manner of ways to avoid tackling a particular task we might not be excited about or are just plain terrified of doing. This can especially be the case when you are coming up to writing about a tough time in your life.

It is best to take these components on first! With the toughest stuff out of the way early, it clears the path for you to breeze through the rest.

Knowing your book's purpose and remembering why you were called to write in the first place are some of the best motivators to staying the course with your first draft.

There is really no such thing as multitasking. It is simply the brain switching back and forth rapidly between two tasks. The result? More stress for you, and each chore taking more than twice as long compared with working on each thing one at a time. When you sit down to write – make that your sole focus.

Beating writer's block

You will be surprised by how much you can achieve when you are free of distraction.

The more you sit down to write, the quicker your mind gets used to switching into creation mode. You can help this along and maximise the time you have to create by paying attention to how you get into 'flow'. We've mentioned small rituals you can use to get yourself into a creative state when you begin. There are others you can utilise when you wrap up a session that can serve as a way to stimulate your train of thought and propel you back into flow at a faster rate when you come back.

You could try using Ernest Hemingway's technique of ending every session with a half-finished sentence so that when you start the next session, you can easily jump back into your train of thought. He is quoted as saying, 'The best way is always to stop when you are going good and when you know what will happen next. If you do that every day... you will never be stuck. That way your subconscious will work on it all the time. But if you think about it consciously or worry about it you will kill it and your brain will be tired before you start.'[12] Of course, he was writing fiction, but this strategy is just as effective for nonfiction writing too.

Or perhaps writing yourself a little post-it note or hint in your document that you can leave in order to trigger a thought or remind yourself what you had in mind for the next session.

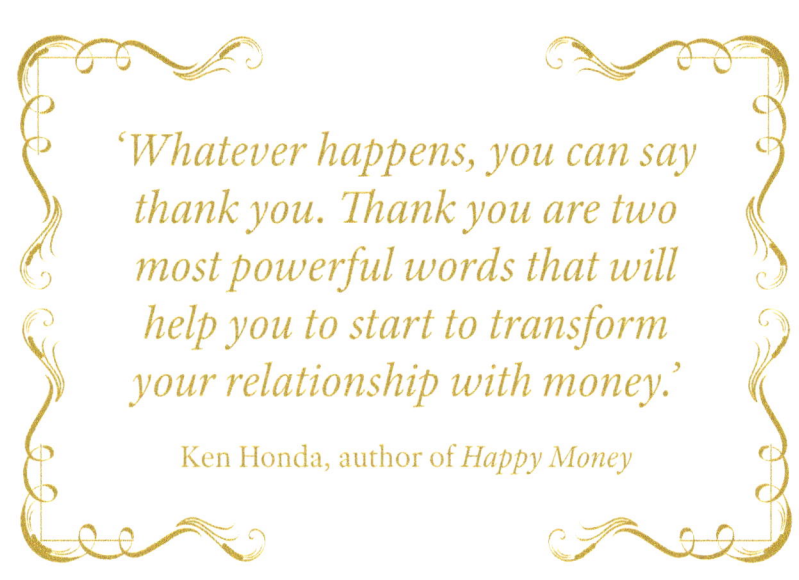

'Whatever happens, you can say thank you. Thank you are two most powerful words that will help you to start to transform your relationship with money.'

Ken Honda, author of *Happy Money*

Product vs pillar

Ignite & Write: The Structured Author

It is common for aspiring authors to get caught up in writing and publishing their books and forget to build a following and an audience. Even worse is when authors don't realise the potential their book has to make money... and I'm not talking about book sales!

There is an old paradigm that to be a creative means you have to struggle. That stereotype that you have to sacrifice earning good money in order to pursue your creative passion needs to go. In fact, it may be a barrier for many people who want to write because they fail to see the monetary value in pursuing their creative endeavours.

I will never forget sitting in a community hall in 2019 and listening to a prominent crime author on a national tour for what would have been his eleventh novel. We had reached the Q and A portion of the evening, and someone asked him if he earned a decent income as an author. He replied that when he added up all of the hours he invested in research, writing and rewriting his books, his annual earnings would be equivalent to the minimum wage.

The reason for this? He was relying solely on book sales.

According to research released in 2022 conducted by Macquarie University for the Australia Council for the Arts and the Copyright Agency, the average annual income of an Australian author is only $18,200.[13] This has left two-fifths of authors relying on their partner's income and another two-fifths relying on a day job that is unrelated to their writing.

Product vs pillar

It's no secret that for most of us mere mortals, publishing your book won't automatically make you wealthy. For those who hit the sweet spot of releasing a book to the market in the perfect conditions with the perfect amount of publicity and the perfect amount of hype, it could open up a lucrative career as an author. For the rest of us, it may take a little more work to reach the dizzying heights of literary fame.

> Never say never! If you do the preparation and take the marketing of your book seriously, you can truly pave the way to make a serious impact.

But when it comes to making money from your book, all it takes is a simple mindset shift. Instead of thinking of your book as a *product* that has a value of $20 to $25, it's time to recognise your book as a powerful *pillar*. You can use this pillar to build just about anything!

Where will you take it?

Can you already identify how you can include some subtle calls to action throughout your book? Calls to action that plant the seed for ways in which readers can extend their connection to you? Full disclosure, there are some in this very book, if you look closely enough. This book is most definitely a pillar for my business.

Ignite & Write: The Structured Author

As a ghostwriter, the one-on-one work I do with each author takes months at a time, and there are only so many in-person workshops I can conduct each year because there is only one of me. So, my online Ignite & Write Course and book trilogy are designed to support aspiring authors around the globe so they can get started on their own journeys.

If you read this book and succeed at authorship on your own, I celebrate you! I also appreciate that you may need extra support to achieve your goals. That's why I offer other services, such as the online workshops and my mentorship program, that provide a more personalised experience. Knowing about these options, you can decide whether you have the confidence to go it alone or trust me to support you on your journey. As you can see, *The Structured Author* is much more than just a book – it's a pillar for both my business and for your authorship journey!

I am living proof that authors don't have to settle for $18,000 a year. Along with running a six-figure business, I am able to work school hours and be a hands-on mum for my two kids. Even more, I have successfully demonstrated that helping to usher stories into the world can be a credible business. In 2021, I won the Micro/Small Business Woman of the Year Award for the Sunshine Coast Business Women's Network; in 2023, I won the Sunshine Coast Business Awards Creative Industries category; and in the same year, secured the Australian ROAR silver award for Best Author/Writer.

There is nothing special about me; I am just like you. All of that, and more, is possible for you too.

Product vs pillar

As an author, you have tapped into a strong internal purpose and drive to put in the long hours to write your book. The key takeaway I want you to have is:

Inspiration + Influence = Income

When your story *inspires* people and you show them how you can *influence* their way of being, they will be more inclined to buy a product or service from you, which leads to *income*.

When you write a book that comes from the heart, people will already feel like they know you. When you step out from the pages and put yourself out there as a person in the world, they will come to like and trust you – it's the golden triangle of business that you can organically bring to the fore throughout the pages of your book.

We know that people often don't buy your product or service; they buy *you*. They buy a connection to you as a person and you as a business. So, you can choose to be brave and use your inspiration and your influence to get income, or you can stay silent and remain the best-kept secret on the planet.

To give you a spot of *inspiration*, I'd like to share a quick client story with you. I have worked directly with dozens of authors, the majority of whom I cannot name due to signing NDAs in my position as a ghostwriter. However, one such author who has made our working relationship public is Stew Darling. Stew came to me with a leadership framework he had created based on his decades of service as a covert operations manager in the

Ignite & Write: The Structured Author

British Military and Intelligence agencies and his subsequent foray into business after military retirement. His framework was sound and sturdy, but I knew it would be his unique lived experience that would be the major drawcard and point of difference for his readers.

By convincing him to open up and share some stories that wouldn't compromise national security, we were able to create a different style of leadership book that he has leveraged impressively. From the outset, Stew knew this book was going to be a pillar for his business and would establish his credibility as an industry leader. He used his book to:

- launch nation-wide leadership forums across New Zealand
- expand his business to bring on staff
- gain his own weekly radio show where he connects with leaders around the world and shares their stories – enhancing his profile even further
- become a respected leadership commentator in the New Zealand mainstream media.

All of this from having the bravery to step up, tell his story and know that the value of his book was not just in book sales. At the time of writing, Stew had also released his second book, *Unstoppable Force*, and is embodying that message every single day.

An author who has become a global force in publishing is Kim McCosker. Kim has created a business empire off the back of a single book – *4 Ingredients*. This book was released at a

Product vs pillar

time when celebrity chefs were using increasingly gourmet ingredients and complicated cooking techniques. It was designed to show households how to cook delicious meals with four basic ingredients, no consommé or cassoulet in sight.

Kim now has forty-one cookbooks with global sales of over ten million, ebooks, apps, TV shows, tens of thousands of recipes, images, videos, manuscripts and databases with a reach of millions. There is a 4 Ingredients range of kitchenware, and both Kim and the 4 Ingredients brand have won more local, national and international business awards than I have time to list here.

All off the back of a single book!

So, how can you start to have influence?

There are three major ways:

1. Influence within the pages.
2. Influence outside the pages.
3. Influence through other platforms.

Influence within the pages

There are powerful stories that can be told, and once the reader finishes the final page, they are profoundly changed. Your powerful story has sparked something in them. Something that tells them they want to make a change and they need help to make it happen.

There are powerful tools that you can implement within the pages of your book that can subtly guide the reader towards ways in which you can help or support them going forward. Think about how you can add leverage points within its pages so your book becomes a pillar to make you more money in the future.

Instead of thinking about it as 'selling,' which is a hardline stance, think of it as using your book to maximise the opportunity for your reader to transform and make long-lasting and positive changes to their health, mindset, wellbeing, financial situation, creativity, whatever it may be for you.

I have included *all* of these elements in my books, but you can pick and choose what might work well for you.

 Seeding

If you already have an established business or program that can support your reader beyond the pages of the book, make sure you 'seed' or mention this in relevant stages of your book. It is a gentle way of marketing to your readers while also letting them take comfort in knowing that more support is available to them should they need it.

Financial advisor Scott Pape is the master of this! Throughout his book, *The Barefoot Investor*, you will find references to people's personal experiences and invitations to join a subscription-based membership program that has a low entry price point but hundreds of thousands of members.

Product vs pillar

For me, it was about assuring my readers that I have the Ignite & Write Workshops and Mentorship programs available if they require hands-on support and guidance. Alternatively, they can tap into my ghostwriting service if the thought of writing feels overwhelming.

 Interactive elements

If you have other elements that you would like your reader to experience, you can include these in your book. Shari Hall's *Perfect Love* is one of my favourites for this. We worked through a draft of her memoir, and she was going to include CDs with books purchased so people could hear the songs behind the stories she was sharing. Instead, I suggested she include QR codes so readers could go straight to the relevant song in her catalogue and listen to it while reading the story behind the lyrics in the book. It was a powerful way to combine her music with her book and is something her readers have loved interacting with.

 Downloadable content

If you have worksheets or activities you would like your readers to work through, you can create downloadable content. Not only does this save you on printing and editing costs because you do not have to dedicate pages within your book to this, but it is a fact that libraries don't like to buy books that have working components inside because it encourages people to write in them! Once someone scribbles in the pages, they can no longer use the book.

Instead, by hosting this content on your website, you can dedicate a line or two within your book to let your readers know the content is available and tell them how to find it. You can make it accessible when the reader provides you with their name and email address. This is marketing gold because you can then add the information to your database and market directly to them in the future. Not only will you then know who your readers are, but when you have a new product or service on offer, you can contact them directly, knowing they are a warm lead who already knows, likes and trusts you. Plus, they are familiar with your work.

Author of *The Charge*, Brendon Burchard, is a master of this. At the end of every chapter, he has a workbook or resource you can download.

Influence outside the pages

While everything within the pages is designed to provide a seamless roadmap for your readers to engage further with you, the *real* magic happens with what you create outside the pages. This is where you can really leverage your book to make a difference to your hip pocket and provide extra value for your readers.

What this takes from you as the author is a strong conviction and desire to put yourself out there in a manner that may be foreign to you; then again, it may be second nature. You need to embrace the power of your message and know in your heart of hearts that it is something people need to hear. So, how can you start to extend that influence outside of the pages now that you have inspired your readers?

When talking about her authorship journey on the *Ignite & Write* podcast, Kym Cousins shared how writing *Selling with Heart* helped her to gain clarity on what she wanted to do with her business.

> 'Alongside the writing, I was also working out what I was doing in my business as a sales enablement consultant coach. What was it I wanted to help people do? There were lots of things I could help them with, but ultimately, what was it I wanted them to *gain* through working with me? Alongside the writing, I was building my business. What was my product? What was my service? What was my offering? What was the message? I knew I could do a whole bunch of things, but to niche it right down, to be very specific about what outcome I could get for people, it came down to giving people confidence to sell.'

You can watch the full interview here:

Think about what you can offer your reader that adds value to their life. How can you offer support? What knowledge can you share? Here are some ways in which you can bring your ideas to life and expand on the content of your book in order to better support your readers who want to become clients:

Ignite & Write: The Structured Author

 One-to-one or 'done for you' service

If you take a leaf out of my journey, I started with a one-to-one ghostwriting model where I would literally work with one client over a four-month period. I had an attitude of go hard or go home. It remains my highest-end offer for clients. When your book has a strong theme or message that is linked to something people may need hands-on support with, this 'done for you' service is a way to support them in a nurturing and private environment. Do note, though, that your time is valuable, and you will need to set your pricing to reflect that.

 Workshops

This was the second element I introduced into my business model. It allowed me to offer a one-to-many model, which is great for business scale. Instead of taking on the heavy load of writing for my clients, I discovered there is a large cohort of people who get great satisfaction from writing their own books. They just need a little help to do that. I keep my workshops intimate with a higher price point because I value that, but you could look at lower price points and fill up a larger room to teach your content.

 Mentorships/group programs

This is the step between my workshops and ghostwriting, as there were people who left the workshops super pumped but then became deflated during the writing process and left their manuscripts by the wayside, incomplete. My Ignite & Write Mentorship is a twelve-week program that supports people through the writing process and provides participants with accountability, all in a group setting alongside like-minded people. Mentorships or group programs can work for just about any theme you can think of – you could create a weight loss challenge, a financial overhaul program or even coach people through how to create their own fictional characters or worlds through development programs.

These can be done online or in person.

 Speaking

For the bold, getting yourself out there in front of other people's audiences is *the* number one quickest way to boost your profile and create awareness around your book and the business you have built around it. It takes courage, but because you are so connected with the power of your story, I know you can find the confidence to do this! You can start small with groups or organisations you are familiar with, and when the shakes disperse, you can reach out to brands and tap into their ready-made audiences.

This does not necessarily mean you have to prepare keynote speeches off the bat. Still, something as simple as showing up and reading an excerpt of your book (or the whole one if it's a picture book) can introduce you and your work to a range of people who wouldn't have otherwise known you. This is something my son has done with his book, *Sprout's Idea*. In fact, his whole book was premised on a story he imagined for a music festival where he got up in front of a crowd of more than 100 people – he was only eight at the time – and read it out. If he can do it, anyone can put their big-person pants on and do the same!

Practice makes perfect with this, believe me, but if I can go from being a timid journalist, too scared to speak up and ask a single question at a press conference (where the focus isn't even on me), to not even getting the shakes when I'm at my book launch with close to 100 people in the room, anyone can do it.

It is lucrative when you get into the right circles. If you want to pursue speaking as a major component of your book business, consistency and experience can lead to charging thousands for a single engagement, which can become the top of your ladder.

 Online community

If you have more time or unbridled passion for your theme, you could look at building an online or in-person community that provides a platform for people to connect and bond over the theme. This could be a free or paid opportunity, but you know the people who show up are part of the community you wish to connect with.

 Book

Don't forget that your book itself is a resource. Reminding people of why they should buy a copy and the value that lies within the pages gets people onto that first step in your ladder. Because readers have spent money with you, even if it is only $25, they have shown a connection to you and this makes it easier for them to progress up the ladder when they are ready to move to the next rung.

Product vs pillar

This is exactly why Erin Barnes, author of *The Whole Life Success Planner*, released her product. She shared her thoughts on the *Ignite & Write* podcast when it was still called *The Phoenix Phenomenon*.

> 'I've got three online programs, reset programs... so the planner blends with that. It's [the client's] personal accountability on what they're learning outside of it. Corporate wellbeing, or workplace wellness, has become this thing that's so unaffordable for so many small businesses. I want to make health and wellbeing affordable. So [the planner] is this tool that starts the process with people; they can do it on their terms and it's affordable in workplaces. It's certainly my first place to go with people so they can experience the process, which is lovely, rather than just saying, 'You know what? Sit one-to-one, and let me ask you all about your deepest, darkest secrets.' It's like the first step in any of my work.'

You can watch the full interview here:

 Influence

Keep putting yourself out there! The harder you work, the luckier you are, and the more opportunities will come your way. If I had not created that workshop rung a couple of years ago, I would still be a ghostie working from home every day and would never get to meet and interact with incredible creatives. Keep putting out messages that are linked with your themes, knowledge, experiences and values, and you will become magnetic to the people who need to hear your message. Even if you are still in the writing stage, this is something you can do right now. Be more conscious of what you are posting on your social media, and start to angle your content towards themes that match your future book. This means the people who engage with you online will already be connected to your message and, therefore, eager to learn or hear more from you on that topic. This is a nice, organic way to build your community. Bear in mind that this was something I built over several years, but I hope it gives you some inspiration for where you can take it and how much more you can make from your book!

Influence through other platforms

This is just a small taste of what is covered in my third book, *The Published Author*, which has a heavy focus on how to market your book. If you fail to think about how you will market your book, you are doing a huge disservice to yourself and what you are creating. So, for now, here is a little snippet of things you can start to think about in order to uncover the marketing potential of your book.

Traditional media

Love it or loathe it, print, radio and TV remain one of the easiest ways to get your message out to the masses with minimal effort on your part.

Product vs pillar

The trick to securing coverage is to make sure you have a *hook*. With thousands of books released in Australia alone each year, just the fact you have written and released a book is not enough. Even traditionally published books are marketed with a hook – something that is a unique selling point that makes it desirable. Perhaps, something a little out of the ordinary.

A great example of this comes from my own son, Lincoln Rawlins. He published *Sprout's Idea*, a children's picture book, at the age of eight, making him one of Australia's youngest authors. That is a hook that has resulted in him gaining print, radio and television exposure. In 2023, he was even asked by Bonza Airlines to join the pyjama party in the sky they created to celebrate the maiden flight from the Sunshine Coast in Queensland to Darwin in the Northern Territory. Lincoln's role was to read *Sprout's Idea* as a bedtime story to the passengers.

Not only was this a priceless experience for Lincoln, but it exposed him to a captive audience of 200 people. Luckily, they were more than happy to be read to, and he received a thunderous applause. Passengers even asked him to sign their books.

Once you have the hook, make sure you are pitching it to media that is relevant to your message and theme. You might love watching the morning news-lifestyle programs, but if your subject matter is finance and accounting, you are better off pitching it to a harder news outlet.

When it comes to pitching your story to the media, remember that relevance and timeliness also come into play. For example, start to think about how you can leverage already established awareness days and traditions to make it timely for the media and not just another event vying for their attention. For example, it is no accident that I released *The Mindful Author* right before Book Week. Following this tip will make you more attractive to media and pressure them to act quickly if they are interested.

Pay attention to:

- holidays or annual events that are relevant for your theme
- awareness months, weeks or days for your theme.

Remember, 'media' is now much more than the traditional trilogy of radio, TV and newspapers.

 Non-traditional media

This form of media includes ezines, magazines, blogs, podcasts, YouTube channels, streaming services and social media platforms.

These services provide many more opportunities for you to leverage media in order to get your message out there. Just like with social media, the earlier you start, the better. Securing non-traditional media coverage is another way to establish your credibility with potential readers, boost your following and grow your community.

Keep an eye open for call-outs for contributors. There are a lot of non-traditional publications out there that publish contributed content, so all you have to do is write something to match their theme and meet their deadlines. The best part? All it costs you is your time. There are, of course, a zillion opportunities to pay for coverage, but if you can get it for free, why not utilise it? For this reason, I recommend that you have a selection of high-resolution images of yourself. Platforms that accept contributing writers usually have no budget to send a photographer out to you.

There are many opportunities out there; you just have to keep an eye out and seize the moment when it arises. In the space of a month, I contributed articles to three non-traditional publications, one with a few days' notice as another contributor had fallen through, one with six weeks' notice and another that I pitched and won. You know your subject inside and out, so don't be afraid to put yourself out there and shout your message from the rooftops! This is how people who don't already know you are brilliant will find you.

Being an author is so much more than just selling books. It is about getting out there and showing the world how you can help them with something they need. Remember to view your book as a pillar for your profile and/or your business. When your story *inspires* people and you show them how you can *influence* their way of being, they will be more inclined to buy a product or service from you, which leads to *income*.

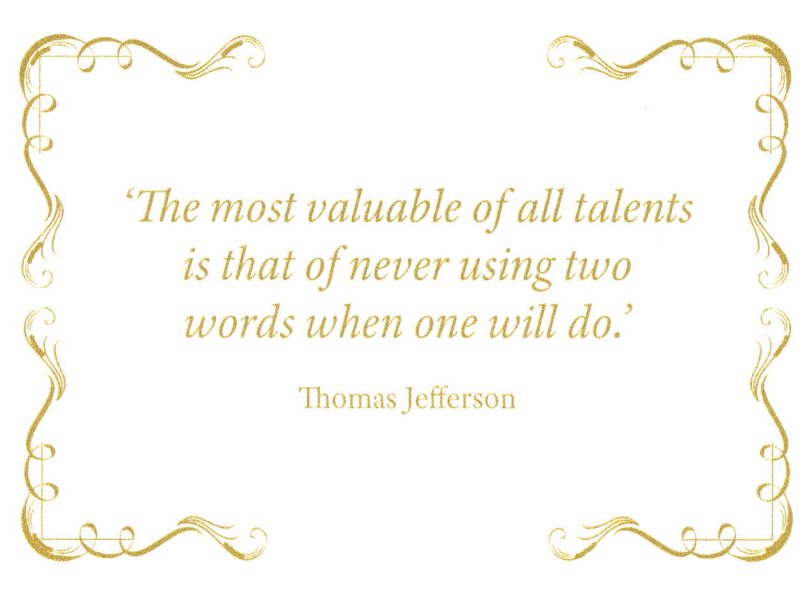

'The most valuable of all talents is that of never using two words when one will do.'

Thomas Jefferson

Beyond the SFD

There is nothing quite like the sense of completion that falls upon you once you realise you have reached the end of your SFD. When you reach this milestone, make sure you celebrate! Tell those close to you, spoil yourself with a meal out or even a cheeky glass of bubbles, whatever you usually do to congratulate yourself on a job well done.

Bask in this glory for at least a week! You deserve it.

Then, it's time to move on to the next steps.

A snapshot of the publishing journey

The road to self-publishing or engaging a hybrid/independent publisher is covered in greater detail in *The Published Author*, but when you take a bird's eye view, it looks a little something like this:

- Build your structure (you can take the pain out of this step through the Ignite & Write Workshop).
- Write the SFD on your own or engage a ghostwriter to assist you with this journey. You can find a balance between both of these options by joining a program, such as the Ignite & Write Mentorship Program.
- Review your manuscript by reading it in full and making note of the changes you wish to make.
- Write your second draft.

Beyond the SFD

- Review the second manuscript draft and make any additional changes.
- Engage a professional editor for a structural edit to double-check the overall flow of your work. (You could also do this immediately after completing your SFD if you are not confident in revising your own work).
- Implement the editor's recommendations that you agree with to create a third draft.
- Engage a professional editor to copy edit your third draft. They will look through the microscope for sentence structure, grammar and typos.
- Accept the changes you agree with.
- Engage a designer to work on your cover and internal book layout. This is where you choose the size of your book.
- Register the ISBN (International Standard Book Number), which becomes your book's barcode.
- Choose whether you would like to bulk-print physical books, utilise print on demand, release an ebook, record an audiobook or any combination of these.
- Marketing, marketing, marketing!

Revising and self-editing

You have been in your creative mind up until now, with ideas flowing and connections being made. You've likely been living and breathing your book as thoughts randomly drop in and bolts of inspiration come at the least expected of times. Once you've put down the final full stop, it can be tempting to want to jump right into editor mode.

I highly recommend that you now let your book baby rest for at least a few days. Do not look at it or even *think* about it. If you can resist and stretch this out to a week or even two, you will be all the better for it.

Why?

Because it will allow your mind to focus on other things and release the hold your manuscript has placed on you. When you are in the thick of creating, it can be hard to see the forest for the trees. Taking time away from your book provides some much-needed distance between you and your creation.

Yes, there likely will be at least two drafts. Even the greatest authors on the planet cannot nail a book on their first attempt; there needs to be revision, refinement and rewriting. As legendary author Stephen King says in his memoir *On Writing*:

> 'When you write a book, you spend day after day scanning and identifying the trees. When you're done, you have to step back and look at the forest...[I]t seems to me that every book – at least every one worth reading – is about *something*. Your job

during or just after the first draft is to decide what something or somethings yours is about. Your job in the second draft – one of them, anyway – is to make that something even more clear. This may necessitate some big changes and revisions. The benefits to you and your reader will be clearer focus and a more unified story. It hardly ever fails."[14]

By placing some physical and mental distance between yourself and your manuscript, it is almost like pressing a reset button. So, when you go back to it, you are actually coming at it with the mindset of a reader.

I encourage you to keep the editing hat in the closet for a little bit longer and simply enjoy the ride of reading through what you have written without a critical mind. Open yourself up to experience the journey and get a feel for the flow. I have no doubt the editing hat will scream at you from time to time but try to remain strong and get to the end.

This is important because it will give you a sense of what the reader will experience. As you know, it won't be a flawless ride because this is your SFD after all, and there is always room for restructuring and reworking content, so don't beat yourself up if you've managed to pave a smooth experience in some chapters and in others, it's as if you've gone off onto a pot-hole riddled gravel path that twists and turns up the side of a steep hill.

Guess what? It's normal!

This is why you give yourself the time to rework your manuscript. No one ever takes their SFD to the publisher to send it out to the masses. While reading through your first draft, consider the following:

- Are your themes properly explored and developed?
- Do any of your characters pop in without context or purpose?
- Have you identified gaps in the timeline?
- The balance between lengthy and shorter chapters. Do they need to be adjusted?
- Revise the chapter hierarchy to clearly identify, main chapters and subheadings.
- Do you need to add more clarity or context to explain an event or educational point in your book?
- Highlight areas that may be danger zones for copyright infringement or potential defamation. You can then go back and either rewrite these or seek legal advice if you intend to keep it as is.
- Is there relevance and appropriate connection for your ideal reader or target market?
- Are there additional stories you can add (you may have just remembered them) that will elevate your content further?

With your read-through done, you will now know in your gut where you need to make improvements. *Now* you can get the editor and analyst hats out of the cupboard and wear them with gusto as you shape your second draft. I know many of my clients prefer to make notes, highlight, or copy and paste directly into their working files.

Beyond the SFD

Whichever way you prefer, I highly recommend renaming your document and saving it as a separate file, so you have an untainted version of your SFD and then another file you can name something like V2. Adding the date to the file name is also a good idea so you can immediately see which is the most up-to-date version of your work.

Tracking your changes is also a good idea. If you haven't used this before, it is a function you can use in most word-processing software to keep a record of the changes you make to your document. In Microsoft Word, for example, you will easily see anything that has been deleted, copied and pasted to another location, edited or added. The track changes function will highlight those areas every time you click your mouse or place a keystroke.

If you are not confident in reviewing your first draft yourself, you can engage an editor or writing mentor to provide feedback. I get it; this is whole new territory for you, but the last thing you want to do is walk away at this stage because uncertainty creeps in once more. If you cannot bring yourself to review your first draft, find a professional who can do it for you (I know someone awesome, by the way... 😉)

The first step in the professional editing process is sourcing a development or structural edit. Your writing mentor or editor will track their changes for you so you can see at a glance what they have suggested you change.

Self-editing tips

If you choose to edit the manuscript yourself, here are a few style points to keep in mind:

- Check the region your document is set to. Oftentimes it is set to American English by default, which means you will end up with words like 'realize' in your manuscript. If you need to change it to Australian or UK spelling in Word, head to the Review tab, select Language and Australian English set to default.

- When you or another character are having thoughts and you want to convey that internal dialogue, italicise the words they would be thinking, no quotation marks needed.

- Where someone is speaking, choose a style for your quotation marks. Traditionally these would be the double quotation marks, however, it is becoming more common to use the single version. Whatever you choose, consistency is the key.

- You can italicise words for emphasis. Do this instead of underlining or writing words in all capitals, as it is distracting for your reader.

- Choose a style for numbers. In print media, they write out the words for everything up to 10 and from then on, it is numerals. For your book, you may choose to use all words or all numerals. Again, consistency is the key.

Try to be mindful of overusing unnecessary words such as 'that', 'really', 'very', 'just', 'literally' and 'definitely'. Don't stress too much about this, as your future editor will be able to chop any excessive words out for you.

There are a number of great software programs that can assist with self-editing, but I find you get what you pay for in these cases. Free software will not be as thorough. I highly recommend that if you intend to release your book to the world that you have a real life human (preferably a professional editor) review the book before you publish.

With the review complete and your notes in place, there's really nothing fancy involved in writing your second draft. All you have to do is execute the changes you or the professional you are working alongside have identified.

Second draft

Once you have completed your second draft, it is time to turn your attention to the other elements that are important to include in your manuscript. Too often, authors forget about the 'front and back matter' and send their main content through to the editor without this crucial element.

So, what exactly is 'front and back matter'? Well, it's just fancy industry-speak for writing the content that sits on either side of your actual story. This can include everything from your acknowledgements and author bio to your copyright statement. Ensuring you include these final parts in your manuscript before you send everything to the editor will save you time and money, as the editor will need to look at *all* of the words in order to do their job properly.

Too often, I see people who venture off on their journey on their own, forgetting these important components, and they then have to write them and wait for their editor to finish the next manuscript on their desk before they can get back to checking their front and back matter. Yes, it is just as important to have these components as error-free as possible.

I have included the most common front and back matter elements you will find in nonfiction books. You do not have to include all of them. You may choose to have none. Bear in mind that they can enhance the reader's experience, and some elements, like references, are required if you are referring to statistics or other people's content throughout your book to cover copyright obligations.

Depending on the style of book you wish to create, there are some other common sections you can include to enhance the reader experience.

Beyond the SFD

Front matter

Title page

This is a basic version of your cover that goes inside the book and includes the book title and the name of the author. It may also include some kind of illustration.

Imprint

This is an element that your publisher will create when the book goes through the typesetting/design phase. Basically, it covers all of the details of the author and anyone who was involved in the creation of the book. This is also where you would place any important information about the contents of the book, such as:

- trigger warnings
- disclaimers
- copyright notices
- inclusion of pseudonyms
- assertion of the author's rights.

It usually appears directly after the book's title page. Your publisher will likely have a standard disclaimer that they use for their authors, but if you need inspiration for additional things to add according to industry, head to the Ignite & Write Resource Centre and download the Imprint Page Wording document from here:

Ignite & Write: The Structured Author

 Dedication

This is a special mention, usually only one or two sentences, and one of the first things your readers will see when they get past the title page. It could be for the inspiration of your book, your family, a dear friend or even an intimate message for your reader. I have read powerful dedications that have included a poignant excerpt from a poem or song lyric that really sets the tone for what is to come.

 Foreword/afterword

This is a type of endorsement written by a third party and is great to include if you wish to add another level of professional credibility to your book. You can approach someone who is a renowned expert in your field to write something for you. You may also approach celebrity figures who are ambassadors for the cause you are writing about. Don't be afraid to reach for the stars with this!

Remember, the answer is always no until you ask the question. You would usually wait until you have completed the first or second draft before approaching people to write something for you, as they will likely want to be able to read what you are about to release before putting their name to it. Super busy people may prefer that you write a synopsis if they don't have the time to read your book in its entirety, but address this with each individual so you aren't doing work unnecessarily.

Beyond the SFD

 Prologue/epilogue

A prologue can be used at the beginning of your book if you feel like you need to add more context to your story than the main body of writing allows. You can use a prologue to provide background information on some characters, the setting or even events *before* the main story unfolds. The epilogue can be used to provide a condensed update on what happened following the conclusion of the events in the main story and the time of writing. This can be powerful to use in a memoir, where the story might cover a period of time much earlier than when the book was written and published.

 Preface/Introduction

Not to be confused with a foreword, the author writes a preface to lay out why the book exists, the subject matter and its goals. It is your chance to draw the readers in, and you can use it to give some succinct yet irresistible insights into what awaits the readers. Now, this doesn't mean it is a synopsis of your book. You want to leave the journey for later. Instead, you can use a preface to highlight your goal for writing the book. If it was inspired by a particular event or sparked by an unexpected catalyst, this can be a great place to showcase this. By speaking directly to your readers, you can share what you hope they will take away from your book.

A preface is also a great way to show your readers why you have a personal connection to the subject and share – very briefly – credentials that might help your readers feel like they are in safe hands. You don't have to call it a preface either; you can inject some personality into it; mine is called 'A note from Roxy'.

The preface to Barack Obama's memoir *A Promised Land* is a great example of a preface done well. He invites the reader to join him at the end of his presidential run. He shares how he started writing the book while on his final Air Force One flight, driven by a need to record his time in office. He tells the reader how the book is more than a chronicle of what he achieved. It has a greater purpose – to inspire others with his story of finding purpose in public service.

Obama's preface provides such a powerful introduction to the book that it not only hooks readers in right away but has been quoted extensively by third parties.

You can use a preface to reveal behind-the-scenes information about the writing process that might pique readers' interest, what challenges you had to overcome and how your perspective may have shifted. If your book includes a lot of research, you might share how you conducted your research and why you took a particular approach.

Try not to overdo any of this and venture into spoiler territory. Remember, the preface is just the entrée. The rest of the meal will be served when the reader delves into the main content.

 Table of contents

We all know how a contents table works; their function is to bookend chapters. They are vital navigational tools for books that are structured around topics, as the reader can dip in and out of the various sections as they require specific content.

Even if your book is a narrative style, it is still important to include a table of contents (TOC) for easy navigation for your reader. I use bookmarks as my goldfish memory never permits me to remember the exact page I was up to when I pick a book up again to start reading.

If heaven forbid, my bookmark falls out; I will rely on the table of contents to select the chapter I was up to and go directly to that page, rather than having to flick through page after page, skim-reading until nothing seems familiar anymore. Your job is to make life easy for your readers, so even if your chapters don't have official names, still mark them as chapters one, two, three, etc, in your table of contents so they have a recorded page number.

If you use the headings tool I shared earlier in this book, you can generate a table of contents with a simple click of a button. (In Word, select References from the top menu and then Table of Contents from the toolbar.) If you haven't, you will have to wait until your designer generates one for you.

Each heading will have been assigned a level in the hierarchy. So, a level one heading is used for the main topics, and a level two will be used for subheadings. Most memoirs and autobiographies will not require anything below a level one.

When you have multiple levels, simple is best. You may decide only to include level one headings in your TOC, or branch down to level two to make navigation slightly easier for your reader.

Going to level three or four is rare unless you have very specific categories that you need to highlight. More often than not, though, including more levels just makes your TOC cluttered and overwhelming.

Back matter

 Acknowledgments

The acknowledgments are a wonderful way to get your thankyous out in a clear manner. I describe it as your own acceptance speech. If you were to win an Oscar, who would you thank on stage?

Most winners would acknowledge those who inspired the project, helped complete the project, offered support and encouragement throughout the project's creation.

Replace the word 'project' with 'book' and you can see how similar it is. So, if you were accepting the award for the best international book (that has been made into an Oscar-winning movie) who would you thank?

I have watched people get tied up with worry over going to print and then realising they have forgotten to acknowledge someone important. There are a couple of ways to avoid this: Firstly, start early! Keep a little section tucked away at the end of your working file that you can add names to as you think of them. Just jot them down in bullet point form, and you can come up with something to add, when the time comes.

Beyond the SFD

Secondly, instead of naming individuals, you can choose to be more generic. Authors can use sweeping sentences that catch all of their family and friends in one swoop: 'Thank you to all of my family and the friends who have supported me through the ups and downs of life; you know who you are. I love you.'

Boom! Everyone is accounted for. Many publishers would argue short and sweet for acknowledgments is best, but I have seen it all. Some authors write less than a page, while others write entire chapters dedicated to thanking people.

One of the latter was Ignite & Write Mentorship graduate Leah Polwarth, whose book *Letters to Billy* chronicles finding the love of her life, getting married and starting a family, only to have her husband diagnosed with stage four bowel cancer when their son Billy was just ten months old.

It is a beautiful memoir written for her son that shares how she navigated motherhood, becoming a carer, journeying through grief and then rebuilding her life as a young widow. She demonstrates throughout the book that it was far from a solitary experience as she had support from her family, friends and the wider community. So, when the time came to write her 'acceptance speech,' Leah wanted to acknowledge each and every person with a message of love to show how much she appreciated them.

So, will you be a thirty-seconds-and-done speech writer? Or more of an I'm-going-to-keep-going-until-you-get-the-hook-out speech writer?

References

Book styles that include research, facts, statistics and quotes from other authors and creatives will need to include a reference section. This shows that you have done your research and any statements you have made are backed up by facts rather than things you just felt like saying.

Having this done correctly also ensures that you are giving credit where credit is due and covering your obligation to acknowledge the sources of any material you have used in your book.

There are various ways of referencing source material, but because this is not a university assignment or a PhD thesis, you are free to choose whichever style you choose. The only requirement is that you use the same style throughout your reference list, so you may choose:

Author name and surname, *book or article title*. Publisher or website, location or URL, year.

 ## Appendix

An appendix is an area where you can include extra information about topics covered. You can delve into certain subjects in greater depth and provide visuals like images, tables, graphs and family trees. Include anything that is too distracting to the reader when included in the body of the text. Items in the appendix will support your core content but aren't essential to your book. Include them if you think there will be a selection of readers who would want a deeper understanding.

Beyond the SFD

 ### Glossary

When you are writing about a particular subject that may not be familiar to the masses, a glossary can be a wonderful addition to your book. It's like a book's personal dictionary for complicated words that your average reader may not understand. I have also seen glossaries used for slang or language that is particular to a certain country or culture so people outside of those groups can grasp what is being said with more clarity as they read.

While ghostwriting for a social media influencer sharing her struggles with starting a family through IVF, we decided to include a glossary in the back of her book that alphabetically listed all of the terms associated with IVF, endometriosis and the surgeries, medications and practices that surround them. It is another way she can educate readers who are not familiar with these words and definitions without interrupting the flow of her story for her ideal readers, who are women and their partners who have lived those experiences and already know what they mean.

 ### About the author/sales page

Once the reader has finished your book and is completely captivated by your story and message, they may want to know more about you.

I know some people who flick straight to the author page to read the bio even before they begin reading the story. It is not only a great way to show the person behind the words, but it can be an incredibly powerful tool to utilise if you are planning to use your book as a pillar in your business.

In a nutshell, it is precious real estate!

Think about how you can utilise this page to your benefit by including a call to action below your short biography. Do you want your readers to:

- reach out and connect on social media?
- visit your website?
- book in a call with you?
- download a free resource that complements the book?
- buy resources that complement the book?
- engage you for speaking; to facilitate workshops?

The list of possibilities is endless.

My advice here is to keep the call to action as evergreen as possible. For example, if you are someone who likes to change things up and a workshop name or offering is likely to change, don't name it specifically in the book, as this will quickly date it. Instead, point readers to the website, which can change as often as you want it to.

If, like author Janelle Parsons, whom I helped to structure her debut book *The House of Shadows*, you don't yet know what opportunities may open up or what next step there is for your readers, just list a website or social media handle that they can reach you on. Once they connect with you, you can then discuss what you have on offer at the time.

Testimonials

Using your book as a pillar? Testimonials are a wonderful way to add that extra layer of credibility to your book. You will notice that the front of all of my books have testimonials. That is no accident. They are there to give you social proof that I have the experience and knowledge to guide you through your authorship journey.

You can locate these either at the front or back of your book, whichever you choose. Ask clients or people you trust to write a short paragraph, and you can choose whether the focus is on the content of the book or what it is like working with you. I have chosen to include a combination of both so there is a well-rounded view of who I am as an author, ghostwriter and writing mentor.

Make sure the person writing the testimonial gives permission in writing for their full name to be used. Including a first name only lacks credibility. If the person is a well-known figure or respected within your industry, be sure to include their position and relevant title as well.

I am a big fan of photos because it shows the people who wrote my testimonials are real people. However, if you wish to keep production costs down for your book, you may not want to include photos.

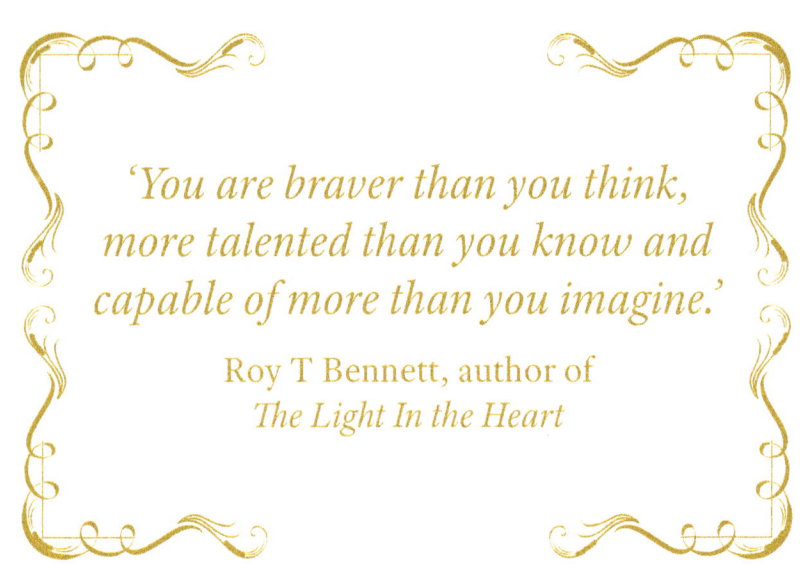

'You are braver than you think, more talented than you know and capable of more than you imagine.'

Roy T Bennett, author of
The Light In the Heart

The pep talk

Ignite & Write: The Structured Author

Picture this: It is twelve months from now. You are standing on a stage, holding a book in your hands. This is not *any* book; this is *your* book. There is a tangible buzz of excitement in the room that fills your every sense. Anticipation and joy in the eyes of everyone around you. They are there to celebrate you. To celebrate your achievement.

You. Are. An. Author.

Your name is printed in large font on the front cover, along with the title that truly spoke to your soul. You have poured so much of your heart and soul into the pages of this book and have emerged from the process changed. You know yourself, truly, for the first time. You know what you want to achieve, and in that room, surrounded by nothing but love and support, you are ready to put it all into motion.

As you officially launch your book and announce to the world that it is ready, you are ready to see what kind of impact it will have and what ripple effect of change it will set off. You feel excited, alive, elated, enthusiastic, sparkling like effervescent champagne – maybe a little bit of nervousness because it's the first time you've done something like this, but it's an *excited* nervous.

As you finish speaking and absorb the sound of applause, you congratulate yourself. *I did it*. You've had the dream, taken the action and brought your book vision to life.

Sounds incredible, doesn't it?

The pep talk

It is all possible for you! Within these pages, you have everything you need to ACT and bring your book to life with authenticity, connection and transformation at its core.

But I'm a realist, and I know that writing your book is not always sunshine and rainbows. There are those little 'friends' that pop up: self-doubt, procrastination and perfectionism. These feelings will do their utmost to halt you in your tracks and keep you small and safe inside the life you know, even though there is a bigger, even more fulfilling life waiting for you on the other side of completing your book.

Writing can be an emotional rollercoaster, especially when you battle with those 'friends' from time to time. Because you have cemented your 'why' and your purpose for releasing your book, you can use this as the ultimate weapon to silence those critical 'friends' as often as you need to.

So, what is the next step?

If you are feeling confident in continuing your journey at your own pace at home, you can utilise the *Ignite & Write Trilogy* and the supporting resources to get you from concept to completion of your book. *The Published Author* is the final book that will give you clarity around the publishing process and share valuable tips on how you can market your book to give it the best chance of making a true impact.

Ignite & Write: The Structured Author

But I understand that you may need more support to see your vision through, and I am not one to leave any aspiring author in the wilderness.

If you feel like you need assistance to move forward with your book, I am here for you! My Ignite & Write Workshops are held throughout the year in person and can also be accessed at any time online, so you can dial in from anywhere in the world (in your pyjamas if you wish) and get everything you need.

The workshop helps you bust through mindset hurdles and guide you through the foundational steps required to build an engaging chapter outline for a book that has the power to transform you, your business, and the lives of your future readers. This workshop is for you if you already have a nonfiction book idea and you have the dedication and passion that require some guidance and knowledge to steer you in the right direction.

By joining the intimate Ignite & Write Workshop in person or online, you will delve deeper into The Phoenix Phenomenon® ACT process, which provides clear and easy steps to build strong foundations for your book manuscript. You will become aware of the inner self-talk that can hold you back from writing your book and become more empowered than ever before to reach your goal. You will also feel more connected to yourself, your story and your audience, which will propel you through any future hurdles to becoming the author you've always dreamed of.

You will have greater clarity of your purpose for writing a book, know how meaningful it is to share it with the world and be at peace with your past and your present, so you are ready to launch into a great future.

The pep talk

The atmosphere at all of my workshops has been electric, and it has been heartwarming to attend book launches for people who have attended and gone on to fulfil their dream of becoming authors.

One such person is Leah Polwarth, the author of *Letters to Billy*, who also went beyond the workshop to complete the Ignite & Write Mentorship program with a group of like-minded aspiring authors.

> 'After losing my young husband to bowel cancer in early 2021, I had the idea to write down as much as I could remember for our son, Billy. What started as just a 'nice thought' and the intention to journal my thoughts was transformed into the idea of a book after attending Roxanne's Ignite & Write Workshop. In just one day, the inspiration and directive Roxanne possessed helped guide my idea into something so much more meaningful and therapeutic.
>
> Roxanne abolished any doubts I had about publishing a book that exposed some of the deepest, darkest thoughts within my heart and soul. The mentorship program kept me accountable and created the momentum and flow I needed to keep me on track to finish what I had started. Roxanne's book, *The Mindful Author*, was my bible and a vital resource for whenever I felt a bit 'stuck'.
>
> Roxanne continuously boosted my confidence and encouraged me to believe that my story was important. Not only was this a book for my son and my own healing, but for all the people I may be able to help along the way by sharing my story.

> I can't thank Roxanne enough for her empathy, compassion, encouragement, and incredible expertise in teaching people to write with true authenticity and integrity.'

Another is award-winning businesswoman Darian Brooker, who went beyond the workshop to complete the Ignite & Write Mentorship program.

> 'Thank you so much for everything, Roxy! You've been such a pillar of strength, support and stability for my writing journey. I can't thank you enough for your expertise, your selflessness and your genuine care and interest in my story and its success.'

If you have read this book and decided writing is not the path for you, do not despair. Words and structure are my jam, so I would be honoured to connect with you to talk through your book vision and discuss how I can assist as your ghostwriter. There is a school of thought that ghostwriting is 'cheating,' but think about it this way – some of the most impactful books would not have seen the light of day had a ghostwriter not been involved. Just because someone has lived an extraordinary life or can move the masses when they speak does not make them a powerful writer.

As your ghostwriter, I will work alongside you to get to know your story intimately, and we will create your manuscript outline together. I will then deploy my interviewing skills, honed since 2007, to allow you to relax and share your content with me in the strongest cone of silence you will ever experience. Your

The pep talk

time investment is minimal – just the planning and interview sessions. The rest of the work is up to me.

I take your words and create magic, weaving it all together into a manuscript that will take your readers on a journey and provide you with something you will be so proud of. You won't be able to wait to stand tall and share your authentic message with the world.

Fashion designer Natalie Blacklock, whom I had the privilege of featuring in *Women Inspired 2023* said,

> 'Roxanne sure has a gift as a writer. She has patience, kindness and a warm spirit and it makes people feel comfortable to open up and be vulnerable in her presence to tell their story. Roxanne then captures it fantastically.'

Authentic voice means everything to me, and if I can have the wife of a Vietnam veteran call me up after reading her husband's book draft to tell me she could hear his voice in her head as she read, chances are I can find your voice, too.

You can find out more about my ghostwriting services or connect with me at www.roxannewriter.com.

No matter which path you take, I wish you every success in fulfilling this dream of yours. Just remember, every small step you take forward will lead to your ultimate destination.

Happy writing!

Roxanne McCarty-O'Kane

Acknowledgments

When you do something as crazy as declaring you are going to release a trilogy before you've even written the first book, it takes a special support crew to get you to the finish line. With two books down and one to go, this is a marathon and not a sprint, but you know what? I've enjoyed every moment of it.

While I may have written the words on these pages, they have been shaped and inspired by the many amazing people in my life. I am so grateful that I have so many wonderful cheerleaders and special people in my life that I could literally write a whole chapter to name you all in an Oscar-worthy acceptance speech, but alas, I can only acknowledge a few here by name. You know who you are, so please know that I value everything you do and appreciate having you in my life.

Firstly, thank you to my super collective of parents: Catherine and Martin, Gary and Sam, and my in-laws Carol and Quentin. I am so blessed to have so many people to guide me through this life. I am grateful for every single one of you.

Special mention to my cheebies, Lilly and Lincoln, who are every bit as crazy, creative and wild as me. You have been my biggest teachers in life, and I am so proud of the way you each are pursuing your own creative interests with passion and purpose.

To my husband Chris – who is somehow still putting up with the shenanigans I get up to with said cheebies. You have provided us with security and an unwavering love that keeps me anchored when my head is so often up in the clouds. Love you forever and a day.

My ride-or-die Candice Holznagel. You have had my back ever since I was an overwhelmed newsroom cadet. I value your wisdom, perspective and your keen eye for catching my many, many writing errors. Thank you for making me look good! You are the best editor one could ask for and the best friend one could hope for.

My coach extraordinaire, Carren Smith, thank you for showing me the magic that happens when you believe in yourself. You have opened me up to a world of limitless possibilities and glorious opportunities.

Illustrator genius Cara Ord, the phoenix you have created for this cover and the two sisters for Books One and Three are breathtaking. Your ability to craft emotive and meaningful graphics has been incredible to watch.

Thank you to Sylvie Blair for lending your extraordinary design talents to this book. Your expertise and keen eye for detail are something I truly admire. It has been wonderful to create this magical book together.

Last but most definitely not least, thank you to *you* for trusting me to be your partner in this incredible, powerful and uplifting journey of authorship. I wish you every success and look forward to being among your growing number of cheerleaders. Stand tall, own your message, and make the difference you have always dreamed of. 📖

About Roxy

Since 2007, Roxanne's unique and multi-award-winning method of storytelling has changed the lives of thousands of budding authors, allowing them to bring their messages to life in nonfiction books with structure, connection to the reader and potential profit.

A prolific ghostwriter, author, workshop facilitator, writing mentor and journalist, Roxanne's presentations are charged with powerful content and tangible tools that remove the mystery from storytelling and ignite a thought-provoking and emotion-evoking theatre within the mind.

Her Ignite & Write series has become a powerful resource for an ever-growing community of aspiring authors around the world to craft their manuscripts with confidence, clarity and a true sense of purpose and passion.

As an MC, presenter and speaker, Roxanne's down-to-earth, relatable, humorous style engages her audience, inspires their minds and moves them to begin to think laterally about their own stories and how their lived experiences and knowledge journeys can have a greater impact on the world around them.

Ignite & Write: The Structured Author

Her emphasis on connection to her authors and honouring the uniqueness of their stories has seen her recognised in:

2023

- WINNER Sunshine Coast Business Awards Creative Industries.
- WINNER ROAR Awards Best Writer/Author Silver.
- WINNER International Reader Views

2022

- Sunshine Coast Business Awards Creative Industries finalist

2021

- WINNER Micro/Small Business Woman of the Year, Sunshine Coast Business Women's Network Awards.
- Australian Small Business Champion Awards Sole Trader Finalist.

2020

- Australian Small Business Champion Awards Sole Trader Finalist.
- Australian My Business Awards for Young Leader of the Year Finalist (one of only two female finalists).
- Australian My Business Awards for B2C Business of the Year Finalist.

About Roxy

2019

 Young Business Woman of the Year Finalist, Sunshine Coast Business Women's Network Awards.

 Australian My Business Awards Young Leader of the Year Finalist.

In 2021, Roxanne was recognised as an ambassador for No More Fake Smiles, a charity that provides advocacy and therapy for victims of child sexual abuse and their families.

To connect with Roxanne, visit www.roxannewriter.com

References

1. 'Buzan claims mind mapping his invention in interview'. Knowledge Board. February 13, 2010. Retrieved on January 27, 2024 https://web.archive.org/web/20100213000356/http://www.knowledgeboard.com/item/2980

2. Lola Badia, Joan Santanach and Albert Soler, *Ramon Llull as a Vernacular Writer: Communicating a New Kind of Knowledge*. Woodbridge: Tamesis, 2016.

3. Maria Leonard Olsen, *How to Become Your Best Version: Wisdom Shared by the Women of the Becoming Your Best Version Podcast*. Self-published, 2022. www.marialeonardolsen.com/books

4. Joseph Campbell, *The Hero with a Thousand Faces*. Princeton University Press, 1949.

5. Christopher Vogler, *The Writer's Journey: Mythic Structure for Writers*. Michael Wiese Productions, 2007.

6. Reinhard Pekrun, *Emotions in Reading and Learning from Texts: Progress and Open Problems*. Discourse Processes 59, no. 1–2: 116–25. doi:10.1080/0163853X.2021.1938878, 2022.

7. The Gold Diggers Podcast, *EP86 MEET ROXANNE – Who You Gonna Call? Ghostwriters*. January 2024. Retrieved from https://www.youtube.com/watch?v=KqWZuQwb7CM

8. Glennon Doyle, *Untamed: Stop pleasing and start living*. The Dial Press, 2020.

9. Tina Fey, *Bossypants*. Little, Brown and Company, 2011.

References

10. Joanne Wilson, *Renovate Your Relationship*. Self-published, 2020. the.relationshiprejuvenator.com/book41416338

11. Crown Law, *2021 Changes to Queensland defamation law*. Crown Law, August 5, 2021. Retrieved on March 29, 2022, https://www.crownlaw.qld.gov.au/resources/publications/2021-changes-to-queensland-defamation-law#:~:text=One%20of%20the%2

12. Mike Springer, *Seven tips from Ernest Hemingway on how to write fiction*. February 9, 2013. Retrieved on April 21, 2024, https://www.openculture.com/2013/02/seven_tips_from_ernest_hemingway_on_how_to_write_fiction.html

13. David Throsby and Paul Crosby, *2022 National Survey of Australian Book Authors*. Macquarie University, November 2022. Retrieved from https://researchers.mq.edu.au/en/projects/2022-national-survey-of-australian-book-authors, on January 23, 2024.

14. Stephen King, *On Writing: A Memoir of the Craft*. Pocket Books, 2000.

The Ignite & Write Trilogy

The Mindful Author

Winner of the International Reader Views Gold Award for Best Writing/Publishing Book and the Book By Book Pub Gold Award for Best Writing/Publishing Book in 2023. The first book in the *Ignite & Write Trilogy* is a resource for you to find your inspiration and transform your fears, roadblocks and self-doubt into confidence and completion. It's time to embrace the mindset of an author and lay strong foundations for your writing success.

The Ignite & Write Trilogy

The Published Author

Book Three is dedicated to what comes *after* you have finished that first draft. Discover the pros and cons of the different forms of publishing available to aspiring authors today, and learn how to determine the best route for your book vision. Marketing is a vital, yet often overlooked, part of the process of becoming an author, and this book reveals tips and tricks to set you on the right path.

To experience the full Ignite & Write journey, complete the trilogy. Head to www.roxannewriter.com

www.ingramcontent.com/pod-product-compliance
Lightning Source LLC
Chambersburg PA
CBHW062034290426
44109CB00026B/2621